KT-370-821

# GOOD
# HOUSEKEEPING
# HOME
# HINTS

# GOOD HOUSEKEEPING
# HOME
# HINTS

BY
GOOD HOUSEKEEPING
INSTITUTE

 EBURY PRESS
London

Published by Ebury Press
National Magazine House
72 Broadwick Street
London W1V 2BP

First impression 1981

© The National Magazine Company Limited 1981

All rights reserved. No part of this
publication may be reproduced, stored in
a retrieval system, or transmitted, in any
form or by any means, electronic, mechanical,
photocopying, recording or otherwise, without
prior permission of the publishers.

ISBN 0 85223 190 3 (paperback)
ISBN 0 85223 205 5 (hardback)


Text: Cassandra Kent
Cartoons: Robert Broomfield


The Good Housekeeping Institute would like to thank
The British Red Cross Society for their help with
the Emergency first aid section of this book.

Filmset by Advanced Filmsetters (Glasgow) Limited
Printed by The Anchor Press Limited, Tiptree, Essex
Bound by William Brendon and Son Limited, Tiptree, Essex

# Contents

# Foreword

It is not easy to define a hint. It may spring from plain common sense, be something your mother told you, or something so strange you would never have thought of it in a thousand years. Not all hints work for all people; what one person thinks of as a wonderful time- or money-saving tip, another may see as a tiresome complex method.

The hints in this book are based on over fifty years of experience, research and testing by the Good Housekeeping Institute. Some of the hints have been passed down over the years and still hold true today; others simplify life in a home equipped with gadgets galore. The hints embrace a broad spectrum of subjects so you're bound to find some that will work for you, whether you operate from a rented bedsit in the heart of a city, or a mansion surrounded by acres of rolling countryside.

As usual with the Good Housekeeping Institute, all the hints in this book have been tried and tested and are guaranteed to work. If you need any help with problems around the home, the Good Housekeeping Institute's staff will gladly answer your queries personally if you write to them at National Magazine House, 72 Broadwick Street, London W1V 2BP, enclosing a stamped, addressed envelope.

# Household Hints

**Airbricks**  **Airbricks or grilles** in the lower part of house walls are for ventilating the under-side of the house to prevent rot. Check regularly to see that they are clean and not blocked up.

**Bath towels**  **Use old, worn bath towels** to make a foam-padded beach mat, or cut them up and sew the good bits together to make patchwork beach towels.

**Baths**  **To stop the bathroom steaming up**, run some cold water into the bath before adding any hot water.

**Remove tidemarks** from plastic baths with a little silver polish on a soft cloth. Tidemarks on vitreous or porcelain enamelled baths can be removed with a little white spirit. Wash off immediately with a solution of washing-up liquid and rinse thoroughly.

**Remove hard water stains** from vitreous or porcelain enamelled baths with a proprietary vitreous enamel cleaner. Stubborn marks may need a second treatment.

**Beds and Bedding**  **Save bed-making time** by using fitted sheets and duvets.

**Putting a cover on a duvet** is easier if you turn the cover inside out. Slip your hand into a top corner of the cover and grab a top corner of the duvet. Pull through as far as possible, then do the same for the other top corner. Holding firmly, shake gently so that the cover slips over the whole duvet.

**Check that a bed is properly aired** by placing a small mirror between the sheets for about 5 minutes. If it mists up, the bed is damp.

**Remove fluff and dust** from spring interior mattresses with a dustpan and a fairly stiff brush. Don't use the dusting attachment of a vacuum cleaner as this could dislodge the mattress filling.

**Cellular blankets** are more efficient at keeping you warm if they are used with an ordinary woven blanket on top to trap in the air.

**When washing wool blankets**, a very little olive oil added to the final rinse will keep them soft and fluffy. For blankets made with synthetic fabrics, use a fabric softener which will also reduce static.

**When drying duvet covers**, hang them on the line inside out to prevent the sun fading them.

**Blankets**  *See* **Beds and Bedding**

**Bleach**  **Household bleach** comes in handy for so many household cleaning operations that you should be able to dispense with some other household cleaners. Check the label for the strength of solution to use for each task and remember that you should always protect clothing, carpets, etc., from splashing.

**Bottles**  **Make use of empty plastic squash bottles** by cutting about 8 cm (3 inches) off the tops and using them as funnels.

**For carrying bottles home from the shops**, sew a strong elastic loop to each side of your shopping bag to hold large bottles upright and to stop them banging together.

**Get the last drop** from an empty shampoo bottle or washing-up liquid bottle by putting some warm water into it and shaking well.

### Brass

**To prevent clean brass tarnishing** and to save having to clean it so often, brush or spray it with a thin coating of lacquer after cleaning.

**When cleaning brass handles** on wood furniture, cut a cardboard collar and place it round the fitting to protect the surrounding wood. Over a period of time brass cleaner will take the colour out of wood.

### Bread bins

**To prevent mildew developing**, wipe over the inside of the bread bin with a clean cloth wrung out in vinegar.

### Brooms

**To stop a broom damaging skirting boards**, stick a strip of draught excluder round its head.

### Candles

**If a candle breaks in the middle**, soften the lower end with a few drops of boiling water and ram the top on, holding it in place until the wax has set again.

**Bent candles can be straightened** by putting them in a polythene bag and holding them under hot running water. When they have softened slightly, roll them on a table top to straighten them.

**Carpets**   **Buy carpet samples cheaply** and use them as door mats.

**Use individual carpet tiles** to protect table tops when using a typewriter or sewing machine.

**When buying stair carpet**, buy it about a metre (1 yard) or so longer than you need. This will allow you to move the carpet up and down to ensure even wear.

**If a carpet has been flattened by furniture**, dampen it with water and vacuum with a suction nozzle to raise the pile.

**Cats' fur**   **Remove cats' fur from soft furnishings** with the flat of a damp hand.

*They were such a bargain, a few pence for a large packet.*

'Bent candles can be straightened ...'

**Ceramic tiles**

**Clean the grouting between ceramic wall tiles** with an old clean toothbrush dipped in a solution of domestic bleach. Put some newspaper down to protect the floor, wear rubber gloves and take care not to get the solution on your clothes or in your eyes.

**When drilling fixing holes in ceramic tiles**, use a piece of masking tape to prevent the drill bit from skidding on the surface.

**To replace a cracked ceramic wall tile**, first scrape out the grouting round the tile, then score a line with a tile cutter or drill a hole in the centre of the tile. Carefully chip the tile out, using a small cold chisel and a hammer. (Be sure to protect your eyes by wearing goggles.) Scrape out the old adhesive carefully and fix the new tile in position.

**Chair covers**

**Before washing loose chair covers**, soak them in cold water to remove a lot of the dirt.

**After washing**, put loose chair covers back before they are completely dry so they can be stretched into shape. Flat areas can be ironed on the chair, but be sure to use a cool iron if the chair has foam upholstery.

**Stop loose chair covers from slipping** by attaching pieces of Velcro to the under-sides of the edges of the covers and to the chairs underneath.

**Christmas trees**

**To avoid leaving a trail of needles in the house**, carry the Christmas tree on an old sheet when you take it out of the house.

**Chrome**

**Remove stains from chrome** with a damp cloth dipped in bicarbonate of soda.

**Cisterns**   **An overflowing cistern** can be remedied by bending the float arm downwards. A worn washer may be the cause and should be replaced as soon as possible.

**As an emergency repair to a leaking ball float** in a cistern, remove the ball, empty the water out of it and tie a polythene bag round it to make it watertight.

**To stop water flowing into the storage cistern** in an emergency, or when you are draining down the heating system, place a length of wood across the tank and tie the ball float arm to it. This will stop the flow but still allow you to use mains' water elsewhere in the house.

**Clothes**   **To stop small children staining their clothes** when eating ice lollies, push the sticks through small paper plates to catch the drips.

'To stop small children staining their clothes when eating ice lollies ...'

**Protect new or newly cleaned garments** against dirt penetration and perspiration staining by spraying them evenly with an aerosol fabric protector.

**Don't wear the same garment** more than two days running if you can avoid it. It'll look good for longer if it's given a rest. Press clothes regularly to keep them looking smart.

**Reduce creasing** by taking shirts and dresses from the washing line or tumble dryer and putting them straight on to hangers.

**To save ironing time and reduce creasing**, put shirts and blouses on hangers after ironing instead of folding them up.

**Prevent clothes slipping off wooden hangers** by sticking a piece of foam rubber at each end of the hanger.

**Hang clothes you've just taken off** outside the wardrobe for a few hours to air before you put them away.

**Keep moths out and give clothes a nice smell** by hanging a pomander in the wardrobe. Make one by studding an orange very closely with cloves until no peel is showing. Roll the orange in a mixture of ground cinnamon and powdered orris-root (about half of each) to give added perfume and to 'fix' the scent so that it does not deteriorate. Then leave the pomander in a cool, dry place for 5–6 weeks until the orange has completely dried through and probably shrunk slightly so that there is no space between the clove heads. The pomander can then be hung in the wardrobe with a piece of ribbon.

**Allow wet raincoats to dry** in the bathroom before trying to brush off marks and splashes. When dry, these should come off easily. If you try to brush them off when wet the chances are you'll just fix them more firmly.

**If damp stockings or tights are needed** in a hurry, don't risk aches and pains by wearing them wet. Blow-dry them with a hair dryer but don't hold the dryer too close if it's a high watt model.

**Before putting clothes away**, empty pockets, zip up zips and fasten buttons. Garments will keep their shape much better.

## Coats

**Freshen up a sheepskin coat** between cleanings by rubbing dry hair shampoo into the woolly side. Leave for an hour, then shake and brush out, out of doors.

**Never hang a fur coat in polythene**; it needs to breathe. Use cotton or silk instead and let the coat hang freely, not squashed between other clothes.

**To remove damp or grease marks from suede**, rub in a little fuller's earth. Leave for an hour and then brush it out.

## Curtains

**Clean curtain rails and poles** easily with a pronged Venetian blind mop.

**Wash net curtains** before they look really dirty; it's sometimes difficult to get heavily soiled curtains thoroughly clean.

15

*'Old nylon curtains make excellent bath-cleaning cloths.'*

**Old nylon curtains** make excellent bath-cleaning cloths.

**Nylon and net curtains are easier to arrange** in pleats or folds and hold their shape when dry if re-hung while still slightly damp after washing.

**Just in case curtains shrink during washing**, let the hems down first, then the old hem-line will be easier to iron out.

**To remove the bulk of the dirt from curtains** before washing, soak them in cold water.

**If you're not re-hanging curtains immediately** after laundering, store them on a clamp-type skirt hanger with the lining facing outwards to prevent creasing.

**Decanters**   See **Glass**

**Drawers**   **Clean baize- or felt-lined cutlery drawers** with the crevice nozzle on a vacuum cleaner.

**To make drawers easier to open**, rub a candle or a bar of soap along the runners.

**Stop cutlery rattling around in drawers** by lining the drawers with felt or thin foam rubber.

**Dry shampoo**   **When using dry hair shampoo**, cover the brush with a piece of gauze or cheesecloth to absorb the grease and dirt.

**Duvet covers**   See **Beds and Bedding**

**Dyeing**   **When dyeing something dark a lighter colour**, remember that you must first remove the original colour.

**When dyeing in a washing machine**, never dye more than half the maximum wash load or less than 1 kg (2 lb).

**Never try to dye fabrics** which have faded unevenly or have scorch marks or bad stains.

**When dyeing**, the new colour will combine with the old rather than just cover it. For example, a yellow fabric dyed with blue will turn green.

**Dye dull or faded bed linen** using a hot-water dye in your washing machine. Afterwards, run the machine on its hottest cycle with a cupful of household bleach in it to clear all remaining traces of dye.

**Electrical**    **Before changing a plug on an appliance**,
**sense**    check that you know the colour coding for the
wires in the flex.

Striped green and yellow = Earth
Brown                   = Live
Blue                     = Neutral

Keep a note of this somewhere where you will
be sure to find it when you need it, such as in
the tool box or drawer with the screwdriver.

**Never repair frayed electric flexes** with
insulating tape. They should be replaced with
new ones.

**Never throw away any instruction booklets**,
guarantees or important information about
servicing provided with an electrical appliance
by the manufacturer. Keep them all safely
together in a file.

**When storing several appliance flexes** together
in a drawer, avoid confusion by snapping on
plastic tags from bread packs and writing the
name of the appliance on each tag with a
felt-tip pen.

**Floors**    **To clean vinyl or rubber floor coverings**
thoroughly, use a rubber-headed car-washing
brush (without its hose) dipped in warm soapy
water. The bristles are stiff enough to clean
without scratching and are flexible enough to
get into corners and round pipes.

**Wipe scuff marks from hard floors** with a
cloth moistened in white spirit. On vinyl,
linoleum and rubber floors, rinse at once with
warm soapy water. On wood floors, polish the
area as usual.

**When using an electric polisher**, dust the floor before you start polishing, otherwise the machine will scrub dirt into the floor as well as polish.

**Rinse floor mops** thoroughly after use with a few drops of household disinfectant in the water. This will kill off any lingering bacteria which might attack the mop head.

**Loose floor boards** are dangerous and often squeak. To cure the fault, use a hammer and nail punch to drive down fixing nails. If this doesn't work, drill holes adjacent to the nails and fix the boards to joists with countersunk head woodscrews.

'Loose floor boards are dangerous...'

**Remove white patches from quarry tiles** with a very weak solution of 60 ml (4 tbsp) vinegar in 5 litres (1 gallon) water. Leave it to dry without rinsing. Repeat, if necessary, and do not polish until all the patches have gone.

**To prevent dust gathering on concrete floors**, paint them with two thick coats of a mixture of PVA adhesive and water (one part adhesive to 5 parts water).

**To prevent chair legs marking floors**, fix glides or rubber pads to their feet.

**Fridges and Freezers**

**When cleaning the inside of a fridge**, never use any kind of detergent. After defrosting, wipe out with a solution of bicarbonate of soda and warm water—about 15 ml (1 tbsp) to 1 litre ($1\frac{3}{4}$ pints).

**When defrosting an upright freezer**, cover the lowest shelf with kitchen foil turned up round the edges. Make a small hole in the centre of the foil and place a bowl underneath to catch the drips. Use an old towel to collect the water that drips from the under-side of the bottom shelf.

**To get rid of a smell** caused by leaving food in a switched-off fridge, place a shallow dish of clean cat litter in the fridge.

**Lingering bad smells** in a fridge can usually be removed with a solution of the sterilising solution used for babies' bottles (1 capful of steriliser to 2.4 litres (4 pints) water). Be careful not to use this solution on any metal parts and wipe the fridge dry before switching it on again.

**Glass**  **Separate glasses that have stuck together** by filling the inner one with cold water and holding the outer one in warm water.

**If a glass stopper gets stuck in a decanter**, apply a drop or two of cooking oil round the edge and stand it in a warm place. Strike the stopper gently, first on one side then the other, with the handle of a wooden spoon, and the stopper should come out easily.

**Clean decanters** by filling them with a warm solution of biological washing powder and leaving for several hours. Rinse and leave to dry upside-down in a wide-necked, stable jug.

**Pick up splinters of broken glass** with a wad of wet cotton wool, then enclose it in a strong polythene bag before throwing it away.

'To get rid of a smell ... place a shallow dish of clean cat litter in the fridge.'

**Grills**   **Save lengthy scrubbing** by lining a grill pan with kitchen foil curved up at the sides to prevent juices running underneath. Throw out and replace the foil when dirty.

**Gutters**   **To help prevent gutters getting clogged up** with leaves, fix a strip of fine mesh wire netting along the top.

**Hair brushes**   **Shine up tortoise-shell-backed brushes** with a soft cloth and a little furniture cream. Any white marks on tortoise-shell need expert attention.

**Wash ivory-backed hair brushes** in warm soapy water, taking care not to immerse the ivory back. Shine up the ivory occasionally with methylated spirit on a pad of cotton wool.

**After washing bristle brushes**, rinse in cold water to stiffen the bristles.

**Handbags**   **Clean a canvas handbag** with a damp cloth moistened with a clear liquid bath cleaner. Rub hard and rinse with a wet cloth. Leave to dry naturally and spray with fabric protector to prevent re-soiling.

**Polish a leather handbag** with neutral shoe cream used sparingly. Never use coloured shoe cream as this could rub off on your clothes when you use the bag.

**To clean out the inside of a large handbag**, use the crevice nozzle attachment on a vacuum cleaner, but do take care to remove loose coins, hair-grips or paper-clips that may be in the bottom of the bag.

**Heating**   **Save on fuel** by making 'logs' from tightly rolled newspapers to supplement wood on open fires and in stoves. Secure the ends with pieces of string and use when the fire is burning really well.

**Clean behind radiators** with a sponge-head dish mop spliced on to a bamboo cane.

**To keep as much heat as possible indoors**, stick foil on the walls behind radiators. Use either self-adhesive foil or kitchen foil stuck to the wall with PVA adhesive. Use a sponge-head dish mop on a bamboo cane to smooth the foil on the wall.

**To prevent discoloration** on the wall above a radiator, fit a shelf over it to deflect particles of dust in rising warm air currents.

**Insulation**   **Save fuel** by checking that the insulation in the loft is the recommended depth of 88 mm ($3\frac{1}{2}$ inches).

**Conserve heat** by lining curtains with special insulating fabric.

**Irons**   **Always empty a steam iron after use** or 'furring up' will cause the vents to block.

**To keep a steam iron working efficiently**, be sure to 'de-fur' it regularly following the manufacturer's instructions.

**Buy distilled or purified water** from a chemist for your steam iron. Do not use water from a defrosted fridge or freezer as it may be contaminated.

23

**After filling a steam iron**, wait until it has reached its pre-set temperature before using it, otherwise it may drip and leave water marks on fabrics.

**Jars** **Turn a screw-topped jar into a flour dredger** by making very small holes in the lid with a bradawl. Make a water sprinkler for ironing in the same way.

**Kettles** **To save fuel**, don't put more water in the kettle than you need, but be careful to cover the element if it's an electric kettle.

**If you boil more water than you need** in an electric kettle, store the extra in a vacuum flask for making your next cup of instant coffee or soup.

**Always empty a kettle after use** to prevent it 'furring up'.

**Remove slight scaling** from a kettle with a solution of citric acid crystals—10 ml (2 tsp) citric acid to 500 ml ($\frac{3}{4}$ pint) warm water. Rinse well before using the kettle again.

## Kitchen equipment

**Hang small kitchen implements**, such as strainers and scissors, on hooks fitted into a peg board hung on the wall or on the back of a cupboard door.

**Non-perishable foods**, such as rice, currants, pasta and dried beans, are best stored in glass or transparent polythene containers so that you can see at a glance how much is left.

**Store flat kitchen items**, such as chopping boards, baking sheets and trays, vertically. If your kitchen has no special tray space under the work top, make one in a cupboard using quadrant beading to hold plywood dividers in position.

**Store sharp pointed items**, such as skewers, trussing pins and larding needles with their points stuck into corks, so you won't spear your hands when looking for them in a drawer.

**Hang brushes, brooms and mops** on various special clips and hooks (from hardware shops) in your cleaning cupboard. This leaves more floor space for things that just can't be hung.

*'So that you can find your oven gloves...
sew a magnet inside them...'*

**So that you can find your oven gloves quickly**, sew a magnet inside them and stick them to the cooker.

**Store a sponge floor mop** with its head in a polythene bag to prevent it drying out. This makes it last longer.

**Clean a blocked grater** by scrubbing with a firm nail or pastry brush.

**Graters and other tinned steel objects**, such as pastry cutters and mincing discs, rust easily so they should be put in a warm place to dry off after washing—a cooling oven is ideal.

**Avoid wasting cake and other mixtures** by having two sizes of flexible plastic scraper which will enable you to get every scrap of mixture out of the bowl.

**Using cooking tongs saves time and temper** when turning food over in a frying pan or transferring it to the serving dish.

**Kitchen foil**

**Kitchen foil can be used more than once.** Clean it after use by soaking in a hot detergent solution and brushing gently, then rinse and smooth it out ready to be used again.

**If you don't own a special dispenser**, store rolls of kitchen foil and paper on rods mounted across the width of a drawer about 2.5 cm (1 inch) from the top.

**Save on kitchen foil** by keeping two widths in the kitchen and using the smaller one whenever you can.

**Kitchen furniture**

**Use the insides of kitchen cupboard doors** to stick favourite recipes, quick conversions and cooks' tips.

**For extra storage** in the kitchen, fit plastic or plastic-covered wire drawers to the undersides of shelves.

**To save space** in the kitchen, remember to fit sliding or folding doors wherever possible.

**Line drawers and shelves in the kitchen** with leftover wallpaper, but do not use ready-pasted vinyl in food cupboards.

**Remove scuff marks** from kitchen unit plinths and stool legs by rubbing with furniture cream.

**Knives**

**When washing knives with bone handles**, avoid completely immersing the handles as water will loosen the fixing material and can split and discolour them.

**Remove stains** from a bone knife handle with a damp cloth dipped in salt.

**Clean stained or rusty carbon steel** knife blades with a piece of wet cork dipped in scouring powder, or with a mildly abrasive scouring pad. Once used, however, their shine will never be as bright as when new.

**Store kitchen knives** on a magnetic rack to keep the blades from blunting each other (or cutting your hands) in a drawer, but hang them with the blades pointing upwards so that if you knock one off it won't fall point downwards.

**If you've mislaid your knife sharpener**, blades can be effectively sharpened by being drawn across the side of a bottle. This is also useful for sharpening garden tools.

**To check whether a knife is sharp**, hold the edge towards the light against a dark surface. Any sparkles of reflected light on the knife indicate blunted or burred areas.

## Laundry

**Always soak an entire article** so that any colour change occurs overall.

**Before soaking anything** in a solution, dissolve washing powder completely or colour spotting may occur.

**Dissolve soap flakes** in a little hot water before adding to cool water for washing.

**Keep woollen garments soft** by adding 5 ml (1 tsp) glycerine to their washing and rinsing water each time you wash them.

**Soak out protein stains** (blood, egg, gravy, etc.) with a biological detergent. Follow the manufacturer's instructions regarding fabrics and finishes.

**Made-up starch** can be added to the final rinse in an automatic washing machine.

**Keep synthetic fabrics clean longer** by adding liquid fabric softener to the final rinse. This also helps to reduce static.

**Iron starched items**, especially table linen, on the right side. This increases resistance to soiling.

**When ironing large articles**, such as sheets, put an old sheet or large towel on the floor to stop them getting dirty.

**To cut down on drying time**, take drip-dry fabrics past the dripping stage with a 15-second spin before hanging out to dry. This should not crease them.

**When using a spray starch or re-texturiser** at the ironing board, put old newspaper on a hard floor to stop it becoming slippery.

**Create a makeshift sleeveboard** for ironing by wrapping a rolling pin in a clean towel.

**If you don't have a velvet pressing board**, put a really thick towel on the ironing board so that the pile can sink into it without crushing while you press the wrong side. **If crushing has already occurred**, this can sometimes be corrected by hanging the garment in a steamy atmosphere or near a boiling kettle.

**When ironing handkerchiefs**, pile them one on top of the other. Ironing the top one partly presses the next.

**To cut down on creasing**, rinse hand-washed synthetic fabrics in cold water before spinning.

**Remove yellowing from household linen** by soaking in a solution of biological washing powder. (Follow the manufacturer's instructions on the packet.)

*'Soak out protein stains (blood, egg, gravy, etc.) with a biological detergent.'*

**Don't store white or light coloured linen** in the airing cupboard as it will go yellow.

**Avoid drying dark coloured items** with light coloured towels (and vice versa) in a tumble dryer as fluff may be transferred.

**To clean the lint trap on a tumble dryer** the best thing to use is a small, stiff paintbrush.

**To test a fabric for colour fastness**, dampen an inconspicuous patch (such as the inside of a hem) and press it with a hot iron between two pieces of white cloth. If there is any colour staining, wash the item separately.

**Articles will dry more quickly and evenly** if the drum of a tumble dryer is only half full.

**To save on water and electricity**, don't run your washing machine until you have a full load. Combine fabrics requiring different temperatures and wash at the lowest. Those fabrics requiring washing at a higher temperature will come clean, but will need washing at the correct temperature every few weeks.

**Always close zips** before putting them in the washing machine so they don't get damaged.

**To dry a sweater flat more quickly**, put the cardboard tubes from rolls of kitchen paper or foil into the sleeves.

**When bleaching delicate fabrics**, such as silk, with a hydrogen peroxide solution, speed up the action with a drop of ammonia.

**When washing small, delicate items** by machine, tie them inside a pillow case. This gives protection and makes handling several small items easier.

## Lighting

**Lighting in a room can be greatly improved** by *cleaning* the electric light bulbs! Switch off the electricity and remove the light bulbs for cleaning. Holding a bulb by the cap, wipe the glass with a piece of cotton wool moistened with methylated spirit.

**Save electricity** by installing a fluorescent light in the kitchen. They're more expensive to buy than conventional bulbs but are cheaper to run and last longer.

**Lost property**

**Keep the family tidy** by instigating a lost property box. Throw into it all the odd toys, shoes and items of clothing you find lying around out of place, and every few weeks send those that aren't claimed to the dustbin or a jumble sale.

**Marble**

**Remove stains** from marble surfaces by trickling on a little lemon juice. Rinse off quickly or it will dull the surface.

**Wash marble** mantels, fireplace surrounds, tables and ornaments with soapy water. Rinse well and buff with a soft cloth. Colourless wax polish can be applied to coloured marble to add a shine, but not to white as it can cause yellowing.

**Mirrors**

**Remove hairspray from mirrors** with methylated spirit.

**Nail varnish**

**To stop nail varnish thickening**, store it in the fridge!

**Ovens**

**Clean a not-too-dirty oven** while still warm by wiping it out with bicarbonate of soda on a damp cloth.

**When using an aerosol oven cleaner**, take care not to get it on a glass oven door or nearby paintwork, and protect the floor with newspapers, otherwise it may become

'Wash marble ... with soapy water.'

---

dangerously slippery and vinyl floors could be damaged.

**Save electricity** by turning off an electric oven 15–20 minutes before the end of cooking a joint or casserole—the oven will retain enough heat to complete the cooking. This obviously is not recommended for dishes that need an exact cooking time.

**Parcels** **When packing breakable items for the post**, wrap them in damp newspaper. As this dries it will form a protective shell.

**Pastry** **Clean your pastry board** quickly by sprinkling
**boards** it liberally with salt and rubbing with the palm of your hand to loosen any remaining bits of pastry. Wash and rinse as usual.

**Pipes**    **Thaw frozen pipes** with cloths wrung out in hot water, or by playing a hair dryer along them. If you don't know where the block is, start warming the pipes close to the cold water tank and work outwards. If you do know where the frozen blockage is and the pipe is not plastic, put a hot water bottle on it until the blockage has cleared.

**Make a temporary repair to a burst pipe** using a bandage from the medicine box and epoxy resin adhesive. Mix the adhesive and spread some on the pipe and on the bandage. Wrap the bandage round the pipe, adding more adhesive as you go. Remember to wear rubber gloves to protect your hands.

**Polished wood surfaces**    **When polishing**, hold the duster or cloth in both hands and buff backwards and forwards for a good shine.

**Take a build-up of old polish off furniture** by rubbing with a cloth wrung out in a solution of 300 ml ($\frac{1}{2}$ pint) vinegar in 1.75 litres (4 pints) warm water.

**Make a soft polishing pad** from an envelope of cotton fabric. Fill this with cut-up nylon tights or stockings and stitch it up. This can be washed and re-used.

**Hide scratches** on furniture with a similar coloured wax crayon. Polish as usual after applying.

**White marks caused by heat or alcohol** can often be removed from furniture with metal polish. Put some polish on a soft cloth and rub briskly along the mark.

**Treat a small dent on a polished surface** by laying damp cotton wool over it for a couple of hours, causing the wood to swell. Remove wax polish with methylated spirit from the area before treating.

**To remove a blister on a veneered surface**, cut through it carefully with a sharp knife. Place damp cotton wool on the surface to soften the veneer, then carefully work PVA glue under the blister. Flatten the blister and clamp or weight it down until the glue is dry.

**Pots and Pans**   **Pans and casseroles are easier to wash up** if you put them in water to soak immediately after use, especially if something has been burned on the bottom.

**Wash glazed earthenware** in hot detergent suds immediately after use. Stuck-on food can be removed by soaking. **For unglazed earthenware**, add a little salt or vinegar to the hot water—do not use detergent or soap.

**Never leave an empty non-stick pan** over a lighted gas burner, switched on electric hot plate or any other heat source. Without fat or liquid in it, the heat will cause the non-stick coating to deteriorate.

**Aluminium pans are easier to clean** if about 15 ml (1 tbsp) borax is added to the water.

**Stubborn stains** remaining on ovenglass dishes after soaking can be removed with a cream cleanser.

**Radiators**   *See* **Heating**

*'Stop your nails piercing new rubber gloves...'*

**Rubber gloves**

**Stop your nails piercing new rubber gloves** by putting little bits of cotton wool in the fingertips.

**Keep rubber gloves tidy and dry** by clipping the gauntlets in a plastic clothes peg attached with string to a wall hook near the sink.

**Rugs**

**To stop a rug slipping on a polished floor**, brush several 2.5-cm (1-inch) wide strips of latex adhesive across the back, allowing it to dry thoroughly before putting the rug down on the floor.

**When an old rug or carpet starts to curl up** at the edges and become dangerous, take it up and coat the back with glue size. Let it dry before replacing.

**Safety pins**

**Keep loose safety pins together** on a loop made with a pipe cleaner.

**Sewing sense** **When hand-sewing with double thread**, knot each end separately to prevent twisting.

**To cut down on future purchases** of buttons and zips, start collecting them from discarded clothes.

**When dress-making with slippery fabrics**, use a bar of soap as a pin cushion to give the pins a better grip.

**Keep cotton reels tidy** by threading them on to a knitting needle or skewer with a cork on the end to hold them on.

**Picking up stray pins and needles** can take ages, so keep a small magnet in your work-basket.

**Buttons will stay on longer** if you sew each pair of holes separately.

'When dress-making with slippery fabrics, use a bar of soap as a pin cushion...'

**When machine-sewing PVC**, cover the shiny surface with tissue paper held in place with sticky tape or paper-clips (not pins), to stop the fabric slipping.

**Curly weaves**, like mohair or terry towelling, can often loop themselves round parts of a sewing machine needle and foot and get tangled. Keep a sheet of tissue paper between the foot and the fabric while you work and tear it away afterwards.

**When sewing with PVC**, use paper-clips and sticky tape instead of pinning and basting.

**Shoe brushes**

**To clean a dirty shoe brush**, stand the bristles in a saucer of white spirit to dissolve the polish deposit, then wash and rinse. Dry by standing the brush on its side in a current of air.

**Shopping lists**

**To make shopping easier**, write your list in the order in which you will buy things. That way, you're less likely to forget things, too!

**Showers**

**Clean soap deposits from shower curtains** by soaking them in warm water in which you have dissolved 30 ml (2 tbsp) water softener. Rinse and wipe dry.

**Silver**

**Black spots on silver** can be removed by immersion in a hot, strong salt solution. Rinse, dry and use silver polish as usual.

**Clean silver cutlery quickly** by putting a 10-cm (4-inch) wide strip of kitchen foil across the bottom of a plastic bowl, and then laying the silver on top of it. Add a handful of washing soda and cover with hot water. Once the bubbling has stopped, rinse the silver and buff up with a soft cloth. Do not use this method for cleaning silver plate if the plating is wearing very thin.

**Sinks**  **If you must pour fat down the sink**, follow it instantly with a pan of very hot water or run the hot tap for a few minutes. If your sink is already blocked with solidified fat, pour down boiling water from the kettle to clear the blockage in the pipe.

**Avoid emptying** tea leaves, vegetable scraps, fat or breadcrumbs down the sink—this doesn't do the drainage system any good. Every so often, tip a pail of hot water with a handful of washing soda added down the kitchen waste.

**To clean a sink**, fill it with hot water and add a few drops of household bleach. Wearing rubber gloves, pull out the plug and replace it upside-down. The water will drain away slowly, thoroughly cleaning the overflow and plug holes, and the under-side of the plug (a neglected area) will also be cleaned. Rinse thoroughly.

**Remove stains from a stainless steel sink** with a proprietary stainless steel cleaner.

**Soap**  **Soap will last longer** if it is stored for some time before use in a dry, warm place, such as the airing cupboard. Buy it in bulk when it's on offer or in a sale.

**Make leftover bits of soap** into soap jelly. When you have enough to fill a 600-ml (1-pint) measure, cut them up and mix with 600 ml (1 pint) boiling water and 5 ml (1 tsp) borax. Stir until the soap dissolves, pour it into a jar and leave until cold. Use as ordinary soap.

**Stop soap kept on a wet surface dissolving** by putting it on a 'soap-saver plate' (from the chemist) or using a florists' pinholder to hold it just off the surface.

**Sponges**  **Soak a slimy sponge** for an hour or two in water containing a little vinegar—about 15 ml (1 tbsp) per 600 ml (1 pint)—before washing it thoroughly.

**Steel wool**  **To stop pieces of steel wool going rusty**, store them in a jar of soapy water.

'Soak a slimy sponge... in water containing a little vinegar.'

**Sticky labels**   **Sticky marks left by labels** on china, glass or vitreous enamel can easily be removed with a little methylated spirit, white spirit or cooking oil on a piece of absorbent kitchen paper. The soft, plasticine-like, compounds sold for sticking posters on walls are also good for this. Once you have got rid of the sticky mark, wipe over the surface with a damp cloth and buff up with another soft cloth.

**Suede**   **Matted suede** can be touched up by rubbing gently with an emery-board. Use a suede brush to raise the nap.

**Protect suede shoes from becoming stained** by applying a special protective suede dressing to the shoes when clean and dry.

**Suitcases**   **Suitcases won't smell musty** if you put a few sugar lumps in them before storing.

**To make it easier to identify your suitcase**, especially when travelling, fasten a wide strip of brightly coloured sticky tape across the top.

**When packing garments of man-made fabrics**, it is much better to roll them up than to fold them. They are less likely to crease if packed this way.

**Table linen**   **Store fabric table mats** on a clip board hung on a hook in a cupboard. This holds them flat and keeps the set together.

**To press a circular table cloth**, start by ironing round the outside edge, then work in progressively smaller circles towards the centre.

**Taps**    **Clean behind taps** with an old toothbrush
dipped in bath cleanser.

**Water stop taps often become stiff to turn**,
especially the one controlling the mains' water
supply. Apply a little oil to the spindle and
leave for a day or two, then turn the tap a few
times to loosen.

**Teapots**    **Remove staining** from teapots and cups by
**and cups**    rubbing gently with a little detergent powder
sprinkled on a damp cloth. Tea stains on
melamine cups can be removed with toothpaste. Stubborn stains can be removed by
rubbing over with a little washing powder.
Rinse well.

**To clean a teapot spout**, pack it full of damp
salt and leave it overnight. Wash it through
with boiling water the next day.

**Tea towels**    **To stop tea towels leaving bits of fluff** on china
or glass, rinse them in a weak starch solution
after washing.

**Telephones**    **Keep your 'phone calls short** by setting a
pinger timer when you start a call.

**Tooth-**    **Keep old toothbrushes** for cleaning awkward
**brushes**    corners in window and door frames, behind
taps (see above), the handles of small jugs and
vases and the grouting between wall tiles (see
page 12). Clean them first by soaking in a weak
bleach solution.

**Umbrellas**    **Line the base of your umbrella stand** with a
piece of foam rubber. This protects the
umbrella tip and catches drips. It's easier to

*'Rinse tea towels in a weak starch solution.'*

wash a piece of foam than to clean out the base of a deep stand.

**Vacuum cleaners**
**Save constantly changing socket outlets** by using an extension lead on your vacuum cleaner.

**Venetian blinds**
**Wash greasy or very dirty Venetian blinds** in a bath of warm soapy water, taking care not to wet the roller mechanism. Rinse and hang to dry. Protect the bath against scratching by lining it with an old towel or a polythene sheet.

**Venetian blinds will stay clean longer** if polished with an anti-static polish.

**Wallpaper**
**Use rolls of cheap wall-lining paper**, cut to an appropriate size, as drawing or painting paper for children.

43

*'Polish windows with a
pad of newspapers.'*

**Spare wallpaper** makes good wrapping paper for Christmas and birthday presents.

**Patch badly marked wallpaper** with a spare piece torn, not cut, to size. Remove the stained area by spraying with water and gently pulling the paper off. Measure the area to be patched, tear the size needed and paste to the wall in the normal way.

**Remove light stains from wallpaper** by rubbing with a piece of stale bread.

**Use leftover pieces of wallpaper**, or cheap rolls bought in sales, to line drawers.

**Walls** **When washing down a wall**, always start at the bottom and work up towards the top. Rinse each section in the same way. This prevents streaks appearing on the wall surface.

**Remove stubborn stains from painted walls** with neat washing-up liquid or liquid household cleanser, then rinse well.

**Windows**    **Save window cleaning for a dull day.** Bright sunlight dries the windows too quickly, leaving smears on the glass.

**Polish windows** with a pad of newspapers; the printers' ink prevents smearing.

**Stop windows steaming up** by rubbing them with a few drops of neat washing-up liquid on a dry cloth. This also works on the glass doors of kitchen cabinets.

**Clean windows cheaply** with a solution of 30 ml (2 tbsp) vinegar in a small bucketful of water. Apply with a chamois leather and buff up with crumpled newspaper.

# Do-It-Yourself Hints

**Glueing**  **If you haven't got clamps for large items**, use thick string to hold joints together while glue is drying.

**Nails**  **To hold small nails steady when hammering**, push them through thin card. Tear this away when the nail has a grip.

**Painting and Decorating**  **After sanding a surface**, use a vacuum cleaner to remove dust before decorating.

**Before redecorating the outside of the house**, make sure all the gutters are clear of leaves and do not leak.

**Before buying imported wallcoverings**, always check the length and width. British ones are a standard 10.05 metres (11 yards) long and 530 mm (21 inches) wide.

**Never hang vinyl wallcovering near a cooker** as splashes from hot food could damage it.

**Light coloured ceilings reflect light** into a dark room. This is especially worth remembering when decorating a kitchen.

**When wetting wallpaper before stripping it**, use a paint roller dipped in hot water. Adding washing-up liquid to the water also helps.

**After wallpapering**, leave trimming surplus paper round light switches and ceiling roses until the following day. It will be easier to trim the paper to a neat finish.

**When applying aerosol paint**, you will get a better finish after several light coats than after one heavy one.

**Before emulsion painting over wallpaper**, do a test in an unseen place to check that the colours do not bleed through.

**Before repainting**, obliterate patches caused by damp by applying one or two coats of aluminium priming paint.

**If you are unable to remove door handles** before painting a room, cover them with kitchen foil to stop paint getting on them.

**To stop skin forming on top of gloss paint**, pour a very thin layer of white spirit on top of the paint before closing the tin.

**Before using a new paintbrush**, drill or bore a hole through the handle, just above the metal ferrule. After painting, put a piece of wire, or a long nail, through the hole and suspend the brush in cleaning fluid. The nail or wire should be long enough to go across the top of the container and hold the bristles off the bottom to prevent them being pushed out of shape.

**When you have a short break from painting**, for a meal or overnight, wrap the brush tightly in kitchen foil or a polythene bag. This keeps it soft and usable without all the bother of cleaning it.

**When painting with a roller**, cover the paint tray with kitchen foil. This can be taken off and thrown away afterwards and the tray can be used again without cleaning.

47

'Strain lumpy paint through
old nylon tights...'

---

**Strain lumpy paint** through old nylon tights or stockings.

**When painting**, stand the tin on a paper plate to catch the drips.

**After cleaning paintbrushes**, always hang them up to dry. Flick the bristles to shake out any loose ones and to remove any dust or dry paint, then store flat.

**Screws**  **Loosen tight screws in wood** by applying heat from a blow torch to their heads or, if you haven't got a blow torch, drip a little vinegar on to their heads. The vinegar will run into the threaded sections and make them easier to unscrew.

**Shift a build-up of paint** from the head and slot of a screw with an old screwdriver and hammer.

**Before screwing screws into wood**, rub them with a little Vaseline to make them easier to remove later.

**Remember to turn screws clockwise** when putting them in, anti-clockwise when removing them.

**If a screw is loose in an electric wall socket**, make a plaster filler to hold it. Mix the plaster filler to a thickish consistency, dampen the hole with a fine paintbrush and ram the filler into it. Push the screw back in while the compound is still soft.

**Timber**   **When planing timber**, rub a candle along the plane to make it slide more easily.

# Food and Cookery

**Anchovies**   **Reduce the saltiness of anchovies** by soaking them in milk for 30 minutes–1 hour before use.

**Apples**   **After stewing apples for apple sauce**, use a potato masher to crush them in the pan rather than using a blender.

**When making apple purée**, 450 g (1 lb) cooking apples will produce 300 ml ($\frac{1}{2}$ pint) purée.

**Apricots**   **Stone apricots** by cutting them in half lengthways with a sharp knife, following the slight indentation line. Twist the two halves in opposite directions to separate them and lift out the stone with the point of a knife.

**Asparagus**   **When making asparagus rolls**, roll the slices of bread out with a rolling pin before buttering them. This makes it easy to roll the bread round the asparagus without it breaking or splitting.

**When cooking asparagus**, tie it into bundles and cover the tips with a cap made of kitchen foil. Wedge the bundles upright in a pan containing enough boiling water to come three quarters of the way up the stalks so that the stalks are poached and the tips steamed.

**Aubergines**   **Remove the bitterness from aubergines** by slicing them and sprinkling with salt. Either lay the slices out on a plate, or in layers in a bowl, sprinkling each layer with salt. Leave for 30 minutes, then rinse off with cold water and dry with absorbent kitchen paper.

**Avocado**  **To stop an avocado mixture discolouring**, put the stone back in and cover it with cling film, but remember to remove the stone before serving.

**Bacon**  **For neat, easy dicing**, buy rasher bacon in one thick slice.

**If you've forgotten to soak** gammon or bacon overnight to reduce the saltiness, put it in a pan, cover with cold water and bring to the boil. Pour away the cooking water and replace with fresh cold water. Bring to the boil again, reduce the heat and simmer as usual.

**Let bacon rashers baste themselves** by arranging them in the frying pan so that the lean part of one lies on the fat part of the next. When grilling rashers, reverse the order so that the fat protects the lean from direct heat.

**To stop gammon rashers curling** during cooking, remove the rind and snip the fat at intervals round the edge before grilling, frying or baking.

**Bacon rinds make excellent cocktail titbits** when cut into 2.5-cm (1-inch) lengths and cooked until crisp in a very hot oven.

**Baking**  **When baking on a griddle** on top of the cooker, test that it has reached the correct temperature by sprinkling a little flour on the surface of the griddle. The flour should turn light brown in about 3 minutes.

**Batter**  **To avoid lumpy batter**, add only a little milk at first and mix well before adding the rest of the milk. Beat until bubbles appear. Batter made in an electric blender never goes lumpy.

**Beans**  **Fresh French or runner beans** should break with a crisp snap. If they are a little wilted, refresh them by chilling in a polythene bag or container in the fridge.

**Biscuits**  **Keep biscuits crisp** by putting a couple of sugar lumps in the tin with them to absorb moisture.

**The simplest way to crush biscuits** for a flan base is to put them in a strong polythene bag and to bang and roll over them with a rolling pin until they become crumbs.

**Black-currants**  **To string fresh blackcurrants**, use a fork to strip the berries off the stalks or open freeze blackcurrants on their stalks and store them frozen in a rigid container. If you give the container a good shake before thawing the blackcurrants, most of the fruit will fall off the stalks.

**Booze**  **Serve beer and lager rather than wine** with dishes with a strong vinegar or curry flavour.

**For a good boozy flavour** without too much liquid, boil wine or cider until reduced by half before adding to a dish. When wine and spirits are cooked, all their alcohol content is lost.

**A bottle of spirits serves** approximately 15 straight doubles and 25 mixes. A 75-cl ($1\frac{1}{4}$-pint) bottle of wine gives 5–6 glasses, and a bottle of sherry gives 12–16 glasses.

*Actually – it's coq au cider!*

'*Dry cider can almost always be used in a recipe instead of wine.*'

**Dry cider** can almost always be used in a recipe instead of wine.

**Cheap red wine tastes a lot better** if decanted and left at room temperature for 3–4 hours.

**If there's no corkscrew handy**, insert a long screw into the cork, secure a piece of string to its head and pull.

**Bread**  **Revive a stale loaf** by wrapping it in foil and heating it in the oven at 230°C (450°F) mark 8 for 5–10 minutes. Leave to cool in the foil before serving.

**Reheat rolls** (even more than once if you must) to crisp them up in the oven at 130°C (250°F) mark $\frac{1}{2}$. They shouldn't go hard at such a low temperature.

**Use up stale bread** by soaking a little of it in milk, squeezing out the moisture and adding it to mince for a looser texture.

**Make leftover bread and butter** into buttered crumbs in a blender. Fry them or scatter them as they are on to dishes 'au gratin'.

**Use up dry bread** in stuffings. Make it into crumbs in a blender or crumble on a grater and soak in milk or stock. Squeeze out the moisture before adding to a stuffing mixture.

**Make the crusty ends of loaves** into bread-crumbs in a blender and store in handy amounts in the freezer. They can be used without thawing.

**A sliced loaf of bread** can be kept in the freezer and used for toast without thawing.

'A *sliced* loaf of bread can be kept in the freezer and used for toast without thawing.'

**Very fresh bread is easier to slice** if it is chilled in the fridge first.

**To make bread quickly**, mix 450 g (1 lb) self raising flour with 7.5 ml ($1\frac{1}{2}$ level tsp) salt. Make a well in the centre and pour in 300 ml ($\frac{1}{2}$ pint) plus 30–45 ml (2–3 tbsp) water. Work into a pliable dough and knead lightly. Shape into a round, place on a baking sheet, mark the top with 2–3 cuts and bake in the oven at 220°C (425°F) mark 7 for 30–35 minutes. Eat on the day of making.

**For a crusty finish on home-made bread** or rolls, brush them before baking with a glaze made by dissolving 10 ml (2 level tsp) salt in 30 ml (2 tbsp) water. **For a soft finish**, brush the surface of the unbaked bread with beaten egg or with a mixture of beaten egg and milk, or dredge with flour.

**When making bread**, measure salt very carefully—too little will cause the dough to rise too quickly; too much will kill the yeast and produce a heavy, uneven texture. Use in the proportions of 5–10 ml (1–2 level tsp) salt to 450 g (1 lb) flour.

**Butter**

**To make butter curls**, use a potato peeler. The butter should be firm but not rock hard.

**Store butter** in the fridge in its original wrapping, or covered so it won't absorb odours. Salted butter will keep in the fridge for up to 28 days, but unsalted butter will only keep for up to 21 days.

**Keep foil or paper butter wrappings** to grease or line a cake tin.

55

*'Avoid smell when cooking cabbage...'*

**Cabbage**   **Avoid smell when cooking cabbage**, cauliflower and sprouts by adding about 5 ml (1 tsp)
sugar to the water.

**Turn soggy cabbage or sprouts** into a sweet
and sour special. Drain 450 g (1 lb) and add
25 g (1 oz) dripping, 60 ml (4 tbsp) vinegar, 25 g
(1 oz) brown sugar and a pinch each of
powdered cloves and nutmeg. Heat gently for
10 minutes and serve with pork or ham.

**Cakes**   **When making a fatless sponge**, test that the
egg and sugar mixture has been whisked
enough by lifting the whisk out of the mixture.
If the mixture is thick enough it will leave a
trail on the surface.

**If a creamed butter and sugar mixture curdles** when the eggs are added, stir in a little of the measured flour.

**To make creaming fat and sugar easier**, warm the mixing bowl beforehand by standing it in hot water.

**Before using glacé cherries in a cake**, remove the syrup from them by rinsing them in a sieve under cold running water. Dry on absorbent kitchen paper.

**You can make your own self raising flour** by adding 12.5 ml ($2\frac{1}{2}$ level tsp) baking powder to each 225 g (8 oz) plain flour. Sift the mixture together twice before using.

**When cutting paper to line cake tins**, cut several layers at a time to save the chore next time you are baking.

**Before turning out a large cake** after baking, leave it to 'settle' in the tin for 5 minutes.

**Loosen a sponge cake from the baking tin** by placing the tin on a damp cloth when it is removed from the oven. After a minute or so the cake will turn out easily.

**If the top of a fruit cake is too rounded to ice**, cut it off level and turn the cake upside-down. Icing the base will also produce a smoother finish as there will be no crumbs to get into the icing.

**Before putting a cake in a tin**, put a long strip of folded kitchen foil across the base of the tin and put the cake in on top. Use the protruding ends of foil on either side to lift the cake out without damaging it.

**It is easier to get an iced cake out of a tin** if you store it with the base on the lid of the tin, but remember to keep the tin upside-down.

**Use a sunken sponge cake** to make a Baked Alaska. Pile canned or fresh fruit in the middle, top with ice cream and cover with stiff meringue. Bake in the oven at 230°C (450°F), mark 8 for 1–2 minutes and serve immediately.

**Create a decorative pattern** on the top of a sponge cake by laying a paper doily on top and sprinkling sifted icing sugar through it.

## Canned foods

**Save the syrup from canned fruit** (it'll keep in the fridge, covered, for up to 3 days) and use it to sweeten fresh fruit such as cooking apples and rhubarb.

**Once opened, canned fruit and fruit juice** cannot be stored in the can as their flavour may be impaired. Other foods can be kept, covered, in the fridge in an opened can for a limited amount of time.

**Leftover syrup from canned fruit** can be used for making unusual fruit drinks. Freeze the syrup in ice-cube trays and add cubes to unsweetened lemonade when required.

**Improve the flavour of canned whole carrots** by heating them as usual, then draining and returning them to the pan with a little butter, sugar and a squeeze of lemon juice. Shake the pan over the heat until the carrots are well glazed and serve immediately sprinkled with freshly ground black pepper.

**Make canned spinach a bit special** by adding some cream. Heat as usual, press out the water and stir in 30 ml (2 tbsp) single cream, some coarsely grated nutmeg and some salt and pepper.

## Cauliflower

**Cook the green outer leaves of cauliflower** as a separate vegetable from the florets. Cut them into strips and boil in salted water for about 10 minutes. Treat spinach stalks the same way and serve like asparagus in French dressing.

**A yellowish cauliflower** has probably been exposed to sunlight, rain or frost. Only the appearance will be affected, not the taste.

## Celery

**Freshen celery** by wrapping it in newspaper and standing it upright in cold water.

## Cheese

**Make potted cheese** with odds and ends of cheese which, while still fresh, have gone a bit dry. Grate the cheese and mix with a third of its weight in butter. Beat in 15–30 ml (1–2 tbsp) dry sherry, cider or white wine and season with salt, pepper and ground mace or nutmeg. Put into small pots and cover with melted butter.

**Grate any leftover bits of cheese** and store in a jar in the fridge for sprinkling on soups and pasta dishes.

**Store cheese** tightly wrapped in kitchen foil or cling film in the fridge. Remove it from the fridge and unwrap it an hour or so before serving to bring out the flavour.

'To prevent cheese going stringy
during cooking...'

**To prevent cheese going stringy during** cooking, use only a very gentle heat and never allow it to boil.

**Mature cheese is better than mild for cooking** as the stronger flavour will come through the other ingredients more obviously, and you won't need to use so much.

Chicory

**When buying chicory**, avoid any with traces of green at the tips. It has been exposed to the light and will be very bitter.

Chocolate

**Melt chocolate** in a basin over a pan of hot water. Don't let steam or water come into contact with it or it will be spoiled.

**If melting chocolate becomes** sticky and dry, add about 15 ml (1 tbsp) vegetable fat for each 175–225 g (6–8 oz) to improve the texture.

When making chocolate curls for decorating cakes and desserts, use a potato peeler on a chilled block of plain or milk chocolate.

**Christmas pudding**

Don't cook Christmas pudding in a metal basin unless you're sure the basin is acid resistant. If it is not, the basin may eventually develop holes.

If you've forgotten to mix the 'charms' into the Christmas pudding, wrap them in greaseproof paper and push them into slits in the pudding when it is cold. These will close up when the pudding is re-heated.

**Coffee**

When making coffee by the 'jug' method, sprinkle a pinch of salt on the grounds to bring out the flavour.

**Cream**

For best results, whip cream in a chilled bowl.

For a light whipped cream to serve with desserts, whisk together equal quantities of double and single cream.

Bulk out whipped cream by folding in a stiffly whisked egg white.

Over-whipped cream can be improved by the addition of a little milk.

Make double cream go further by whisking it with 15 ml (1 tbsp) milk added for each 150 ml ($\frac{1}{4}$ pint) cream.

Don't waste the cream left on the whisk after whisking. Whirl it into a pan of soup or a jug of milk.

Make your own soured milk or cream by

adding 15 ml (1 tbsp) lemon juice or vinegar to each 300 ml ($\frac{1}{2}$ pint) milk or cream.

**Commercially frozen cream portions** don't need thawing before use in hot dishes, but remember not to boil the dish once the cream has been added.

**Always check the flavour after adding cream** to a savoury dish. You will usually find it needs more seasoning.

**Here's an easy way to make your own cream.** Firstly, sprinkle 2.5 ml ($\frac{1}{2}$ level tsp) powdered gelatine over 10 ml (2 tsp) cold water in a cup and leave to soak. Melt 225 g (8 oz) unsalted butter in 300 ml ($\frac{1}{2}$ pint) milk over a gentle heat. Do not boil. Pour a little on to the gelatine and return this mixture to the pan, stirring. Add 10–20 ml (2–4 level tsp) sugar to taste and stir until dissolved. Liquidize the mixture for 30 seconds in a blender, then chill in the fridge. Makes about 600 ml (1 pint).

### Curries

**Cool down a too-hot curry** by adding natural yogurt, soured cream, milk, lemon juice or potato, or a combination of these.

### Custard

**Stop skin forming on custard** by dredging the surface with icing sugar. Stir it in before serving and, if you don't like very sweet custard, remember to cut down the amount of sugar you use to make the custard beforehand.

**For an unusual effect when baking custard**, put a few marshmallows in the base of the dish. They will rise during cooking to form a meringue-like topping.

*'Cool down a too-hot curry...'*

**Egg custard cooks more quickly** if made with 5 ml (1 level tsp) cornflour added to each 300 ml ($\frac{1}{2}$ pint). This means you can increase the heat without it curdling, but be careful not to let it boil.

**Dates**    **To remove the tough skin from fresh dates**, squeeze the stem end.

**Dressings and Mayonnaise**    **Store French dressing** in a screw-topped jar in a cool place (not the fridge). If the jar's lid is metal, protect it with cling film to prevent the acid in the vinegar pitting the lid and spoiling the flavour of the dressing.

**Improve the flavour of your salad oil** by keeping a few olives in the bottle.

63

**Home-made mayonnaise** is less likely to curdle if all the ingredients are at room temperature.

**Save curdled mayonnaise** by adding it, drop by drop, to another egg yolk, whisking well.

**Dried foods**      **Shorten the soaking time for dried beans** by bringing them to the boil in a pan of water, then steeping them for 1–2 hours off the heat. Drain and cook in fresh water.

**Dried onion and celery flakes** give a quick seasoning 'lift' to soups, stews and stuffings.

**Eggs**      **Test suspect eggs for freshness** by putting them in a bowl of water. If they sink, they're fresh; if they float, they're stale.

**Check that eggs are not bad**, before adding them to other ingredients, by breaking them into a cup first.

**Egg yolks can be stored**, covered with water, in the fridge for up to 5 days.

**Use up leftover egg yolks** to replace whole eggs in dishes. To replace one whole egg, use two egg yolks blended with 15 ml (1 tbsp) water. This does not work, however, where egg white is needed to aerate a mixture.

**Brown eggs are no more nutritious than white.** The breed of hen dictates the colour.

**Stop eggs cracking during boiling** by pricking them. (You can use a pin or buy a special gadget for this.) It is a good idea to salt the water well before boiling eggs, just in case they crack, as this helps prevent the egg leaking out of the shell.

'Rapid boiling causes tough whites and rubbery yolks.'

**When boiling eggs**, let them just simmer gently. Rapid boiling causes tough whites and rubbery yolks.

**To make hard-boiled eggs easier to peel** and to prevent them discolouring, plunge them straight into cold water at the end of the cooking time.

**To peel hard-boiled eggs perfectly**, roll each one on a hard surface to crack the shell and loosen the membrane.

**Save fuel when boiling eggs** by steaming them in a tightly lidded pan. Put 60 ml (4 tbsp) water with 1–7 eggs in the pan, put on the lid, bring the water to the boil and switch off the heat immediately, timing the cooking from then. The eggs will cook in the steam.

65

**Turn eggs in the water when boiling them** to ensure the yolks set in the middle of the whites.

**When whisking egg whites**, add a *small* pinch of salt to strengthen the albumen. Too much will make the whites watery.

**Egg whites will not whisk** if there's the slightest trace of grease in the bowl or on the whisk.

**Get more volume when whisking egg whites** by rubbing a cut lemon round the inside of the bowl beforehand.

**Fat**    **Keep a thick piece of pork fat** in the fridge for rubbing round the pan before making omelettes or pancakes.

**Remove fat from the top of a casserole** by dragging a piece of absorbent kitchen paper over the surface.

**To remove fat quickly from a stew**, pour off the liquid and drop in some ice cubes. The fat will congeal around them. Remove with a slotted spoon and return the liquid to the meat.

**When greasing tins and dishes**, use vegetable fat or lard. They contain no water or salt so are more likely to prevent sticking.

**When using the 'rubbing in' method**, grate hard fat straight from the fridge into the flour mixture.

**When draining fat from meat** use a slotted spoon to lift the meat.

**Fish**    **For an extra crisp batter coating**, add 15 ml

(1 tbsp) vinegar to the batter before using to coat the fish.

**To scale fish**, use a scallop shell, working from the tail towards the head, against the lie of the scales.

**For a firm grip when skinning fish**, dip your fingers in salt.

**Buckling can be skinned more quickly** if dipped into boiling water for a minute first.

**Flavourings**   **When replacing vanilla flavour** with vanilla essence in a recipe, double the amount as the real thing is more delicately flavoured.

**Make vanilla sugar** to flavour custards, cakes and puddings by adding a vanilla pod to 450 g (1 lb) caster sugar in an airtight tin or dark glass jar. Allow a week for the flavour to develop, several weeks for it to become pronounced.

**Freezing**   **Reduce the number of freezer cartons needed** by lining those you already have with polythene bags. Remove the bags when the contents have frozen into an easily-stored block.

**When freezing crusty loaves**, remember that after a week the crust starts to flake off. The bread will be edible but not so nice.

**Fruit juice**   **Reconstitute frozen fruit juice quickly** in a blender on low speed with the measured amount of water.

**Fruit pies**   **When adding spices to a fruit pie**, mix them with the sugar to ensure even distribution.

**When making a fruit pie**, mix 15 ml (1 level tbsp) cornflour with the sugar when sweetening the fruit for the filling. It will thicken the juice as the pie cooks.

**Always stand fruit pies on a baking sheet** in the oven. This will save having to clean the oven if the juices run out.

### Garlic

**To give salads a subtle garlic flavour**, rub the inside of the bowl with a cut clove before putting in the salad.

**To get rid of a morning-after smell of garlic**, eat some fresh parsley.

**Don't fry garlic or spices for too long** or their flavour will turn bitter.

'To get rid of a morning-after smell of garlic...'

**Garnishes**   To make a garnish of celery tassels, scrub the stalks, cut into 5-cm (2-inch) lengths, then make several cuts at narrow intervals down the lengths, almost to the base. Leave to curl in a bowl of cold water.

Make spring onions into an attractive garnish. Trim the root end and all but 5 cm (2 inches) of the leaves. Skin the onion and then cut the green leaves lengthways two or three times. Place in cold water and the green leaves will curl up tightly.

**Grapes**   If grapes are difficult to peel, plunge them quickly into hot water (just off the boil), then into cold, before peeling. Use the same trick for skinning pickling onions.

Remove pips from whole grapes with the curved end of a clean hair grip.

**Grating**   To save chopping, grate hard foods directly into a bowl.

**Gravy**   Add extra meaty flavour to gravy by rinsing out the scrapings from Marmite and Bovril jars with hot water and adding to the gravy.

**Grinding**   When grinding ingredients with a pestle and mortar, add either coarse salt or granulated sugar (as stated in the recipe) to speed up the process.

**Herbs and Spices**   Improve the flavour of dried mint for salads and sauces by steeping it in a very little boiling water for 5 minutes before using.

69

**Dried herbs have a stronger flavour than fresh**, so only use half the amount of dried to replace fresh herbs in a recipe.

**Store dried herbs** in dark jars as light destroys their flavour and colour.

**Make mint easier to chop** by sprinkling the leaves with sugar.

**Be careful not to confuse chilli powder** or seasoning with powdered or ground chilli, which is far more pungent. Chilli powder or seasoning usually contains cumin, oregano, garlic, cloves, allspice and salt plus the *chilli ancho*, a not-too-hot capsicum variety.

**Bring out the flavour of bought curry powder**

'Store dried herbs in dark jars...'

by warming it slightly before adding it to the other ingredients.

**To add a yellow colour** to a pilaff or risotto, a small quantity of turmeric makes an adequate substitute for expensive saffron.

**Freeze parsley sprigs** in a well-compressed bundle. To save chopping, crumble off the amount required when still frozen, and return the bundle to the freezer.

**Remember that mace and nutmeg** are the outer and inner parts of the same spice and are interchangeable in recipes. Mace has a slightly stronger flavour.

**Make a bouquet garni** by wrapping a bay leaf, some parsley sprigs and some thyme in a small square of muslin. Tie it with a long piece of cotton and leave the end out of the pan for easy removal.

**Only add herbs to a slow cooking dish** about 10 minutes before the end of the cooking time so they retain as much flavour as possible.

**Leftover parsley stalks** and celery leaves add flavour to home-made stock.

**Crush parsley stalks** for maximum flavour and add to soups, marinades and stews.

**Soften hard angelica** and restore its colour by soaking it in hot water for a few minutes.

## Home-made wine

**When filtering wine**, use a piece of fine muslin instead of a filter paper. This can be cleaned and sterilised by re-boiling, and then re-used.

**In the absence of an air lock** for wine making, use a small, thick-grade polythene bag and a tight-fitting, strong, elastic band. Affix securely and the gases will release through the band but the polythene covering will prevent vinegar fly, etc., attacking the wine.

**Honey**   **Stand honey that's gone hard** in a bowl of hot water to restore its original texture.

**Ice cream**   **When serving ice cream**, use a chilled scoop and chilled serving dishes so that it doesn't melt too quickly.

**Set home-made ice cream** in individual freezer-proof glasses or containers for easy serving when entertaining.

**Ice cubes**   **When making lots of ice cubes for a party**, store them in polythene bags in the freezer. Spray them first with soda water to stop them sticking together.

**To save time when serving drinks**, use ice cubes with a small piece of fresh lemon frozen into each cube.

**Icing**   **Royal icing will be softer** if you add 5 ml (1 tsp) glycerine to each 450 g (1 lb) icing sugar.

**To achieve the right shade of icing** without over-colouring, dip a skewer into the food colouring bottle and add just a drop or two at a time to the icing.

**If you make royal icing in an electric mixer**, leave it, covered, in the fridge overnight to eliminate air bubbles.

**Make a disposable piping bag** by snipping off the corner of a small (not gusseted) polythene bag. Insert a piping nozzle and secure it with sticky tape.

## Jams and Preserves

**When boiling jam for a set**, add a knob of butter to prevent scum forming.

**For a clearer set**, use preserving rather than granulated sugar when making jam.

**If jam won't set**, tip it back into the pan and try re-boiling with 30 ml (2 tbsp) lemon juice per 2 kg (4 lb) fruit.

**For an unusual and delicious marmalade**, replace 600 ml (1 pint) water with pineapple juice.

**Grease the bottom of a burned preserving pan** with butter to prevent burning again.

**Cover chutney with cling film** before putting a metal lid on the jar. This prevents the metal reacting with the acid in the chutney and causing deterioration.

**Use top quality fruit for bottling and freezing.** Bruised and under-ripe fruit can be used to make jams and jellies and over-ripe fruit is ideal for syrups and chutneys.

## Jelly

**When preparing milk jelly**, warm the milk slightly before adding the dissolved gelatine.

**Whisk fruit jelly that's too soft** until light and fluffy, then fold in two stiffly whisked egg whites.

**To unmould a jelly**, stand the mould in a bowl of warm water for a few seconds.

*'A jelly will set more quickly if...'*

**Before unmoulding a jelly or mousse**, rinse the serving plate with cold water. This will make it possible to slide it into the centre of the plate after unmoulding.

**A jelly will set more quickly** if you add some ice cubes. Melt the jelly in a measuring jug with half the amount of boiling water, then bring it up to the full amount by adding some ice cubes.

**Kitchen paper**

**When using kitchen foil** to wrap food for cooking, wrap it loosely. Food for storing should be wrapped tightly.

**Use kitchen foil** to make a lid for a casserole or to make a saucepan lid fit more closely. It also comes in handy when a shallow cake tin is not deep enough, and double or treble thicknesses can be used, if necessary, to raise the edge.

**Keep your work surface clean** by rolling pastry and biscuit dough between two sheets of non-stick or greaseproof paper.

**Leeks**   **It's easier to get leeks really clean** if you wash them after slicing.

**If you're going to serve leeks in a sauce**, first simmer them in milk or a mixture of milk and stock, drain and use the cooking liquid when making the sauce.

**Lemons**   *See* **Oranges and Lemons**

**Lettuce**   **Don't break up a lettuce** before storing it in the fridge as the stem ends will go brown.

**Always break chilled lettuce into pieces**, rather than cutting or slicing which makes it wilt more quickly.

**Mayonnaise**   *See* **Dressings and Mayonnaise**

**Meat and Poultry**   **When basting meat**, use a bulb baster. It is more effective than a spoon for getting the fat where you want it. It's also useful for removing fat from gravy.

**Check that food in a casserole is cooked** by piercing it with a chef's fork. The very fine prongs don't mark the food like an ordinary fork does, and the extra long handle reduces the risk of you burning yourself on the oven.

**To coat meat or chicken pieces** in seasoned flour without mess, place both in a polythene bag and shake well until all surfaces are coated.

*'Ensure meat browns evenly...'*

**Ensure meat browns evenly** by pressing it down in the pan with a flat spatula so the whole surface is in contact with the heat.

**Tenderise steak** by bashing it with a pounder between sheets of waxed paper. The paper prevents the meat fibres sticking to the pounder.

**When mixing and shaping raw minced meat** with herbs and eggs for beefburgers or meat balls, wet your hands. This will prevent the mixture sticking to them.

**Cut an over-cooked joint** into small cubes and reheat in curry sauce to serve with rice. It can also be minced and used in a bolognaise sauce to serve with spaghetti.

**Kebabs will cook more quickly** if you leave space between the pieces of meat and vegetables on the skewers.

**Reheat casseroles** by bringing to the boil and simmering for 15 minutes. Keeping meat warm for long periods without boiling may encourage the growth of fresh bacteria.

**For crisp crackling on roast pork**, score the rind deeply with a very sharp knife and rub with oil and salt before cooking.

**To slice liver very thinly**, pour boiling water on it, leave for a minute, then drain and slice immediately.

**Canned meat slips out of the can more easily** if the can has been chilled in the fridge for 2–3 hours before opening.

**Before plucking game birds and poultry**, immerse them briefly in boiling water to make the feathers easier to remove.

**Buy whole chickens** and joint them with poultry shears, rather than buying chicken portions which work out more expensive.

'*Buy whole chickens and joint them with poultry shears ...*'

**When buying duck or duckling**, allow 400 g (14 oz) per person. Never buy a duck weighing less than $1\frac{1}{2}$ kg (3 lb) as the proportion of bone will be too high.

**Melons**

**Refrigerate melon** only long enough to just chill it or the delicate flavour will be lost.

**De-seed melons**, pumpkins, etc., quickly and easily with an ice cream scoop.

**Make unusual ice lollies** with liquidized fresh melon or water melon.

**Meringue**

**When making meringues** with an electric mixer, take care not to over-whisk the egg whites. This causes the egg to dry out too much and results in weeping, flat and/or tacky meringues which are impossible to remove from the paper or tin.

**Microwave cookery**

**Keep your microwave oven** on a trolley so it can be used in the kitchen or dining room.

**If there is no 'thaw' control** on your microwave oven, it can be simulated by turning the oven on to full power for 30 seconds and then off for $1\frac{1}{2}$ minutes. Repeat this until frozen food is thawed.

**Cook roasts** in a microwave oven in a pierced roasting bag to prevent spattering.

**Soften butter or margarine** in a microwave oven for 15–45 seconds, depending on the amount. Put it on a saucer or plate before putting it in the oven and remove any foil wrapping.

**Thaw frozen pastry** in 30 seconds on full microwave power, but leave it to stand for 10 minutes before rolling it out.

**When food is cooked** in a microwave oven, the centre heats up before the outside, so don't be deceived into thinking that food is cool enough to eat if the outside appears to be just right. The centre, particularly if it is jam or syrup, could be dangerously hot.

**Dry fresh herbs** in a microwave oven by placing sprigs or leaves between two pieces of absorbent kitchen paper. Leave them in the oven for about 2 minutes until they are dry and crumbly. The time needed will vary according to the type of herb.

**Make speedy jam sauce** or custard in a microwave oven in the serving jug. Follow the recipe in the cooker instruction book which will include stirring the sauce during the cooking time.

**Boil-in-the-bag frozen food** can be heated in a microwave oven in its plastic bag, provided the bag is punctured in several places before it is put in the oven. Be sure to put it on a plate or shallow dish.

**Blanch small quantities of vegetables** for freezing very quickly in a microwave oven. Put 450 g (1 lb) prepared vegetables in a container with about 60 ml (4 tbsp) water. Cook on the highest setting for 3–6 minutes. Chill, pack and freeze as usual.

**Freshen stale bread rolls** wrapped in cling film in a microwave oven. The time required is 15–30 seconds.

**Slices of bread** can be dried in a microwave oven and then crumbed in a blender. The time needed depends on the freshness and thickness of the bread. One minute for two slices is average.

**Milk**  **Before using a pan to heat milk**, rinse it out with cold water. This will make it easier to clean afterwards.

**Use dried skimmed milk to replace fresh milk** in cooking. It costs less and contains less fat but does not always give the same results.

**Mixing**  **When mixing small quantities** with a hand-held electric mixer, use just one of the beaters so that the mixture is easier to get at.

**Mushrooms**  **Wipe but don't peel cultivated mushrooms** as all their flavour is just under the skin.

**Mustard**  **Improve the flavour of mustard** by adding a pinch of salt to the powder before making it up. This also helps to prevent it from drying.

**Nuts**  **Store opened packets** of salted nuts and fruit and nut mixtures in a cool place or in the fridge. Use a twist tie to seal the pack or put it in a small airtight container.

**When you need whole nuts for baking**, store them in their shells in the freezer for a day before use. If you crack them as soon as you take them out, they're less likely to break.

**Crack a coconut more easily** by putting it in the oven at 150°C (300°F) mark 2 for 20 minutes. It should crack itself while cooling, but if it doesn't, tap it lightly with a hammer. Don't forget to stand it in a container.

**To crack walnuts without a nutcracker**, squeeze two together in your hand—one of them will crack against the other.

**To skin hazelnuts easily**, grill them until the skins split, put them in a polythene bag and rub them until the skins have come off.

**To blanch almonds quickly**, pour boiling water over them, leave them for 2 minutes, then drain and drop them into cold water. Rub the skins off with your fingers.

**Almonds stay juicier** if not blanched until you need them. Blanched almonds that have been stored for some time can be soaked in hot water for 30 minutes to plump them up.

**To sliver almonds**, place them on a chopping board immediately after blanching and cut them into strips while they are still damp.

**Oil** **For deep frying**, the temperature of the oil should be 180–190°C (350–375°F). If you haven't got a cooks' thermometer, test the temperature of the oil by dropping in a small cube of bread. It will brown in one minute if the temperature is correct. If there is a haze over the oil it is too hot.

**When frying**, add 5 ml (1 tsp) oil to each 25 g (1 oz) butter. The fats can then be heated to a higher temperature without browning.

**Keep oil for greasing tins** in a small bottle with a screw top and pierce a few holes in the metal cap. Sprinkle just enough oil on to the tin and brush it round with a pastry brush.

**Oil or fat for deep frying** can be kept indefinitely if you remember to:
Avoid overheating it
Strain it after use
Coat all meats, including sausages, with flour, egg and crumbs or pastry to prevent the meat juices escaping into the fat
Keep it out of direct sunlight

## Onions

**Chop an onion quickly** in a blender with enough cold water to cover. Switch on briefly, then drain the pieces.

**When dicing an onion**, leave the root end on to hold the layers together until you've sliced both ways.

**Quick-fry chopped onions** so that they stay moist by covering them with water and adding a little butter to the pan. Boil until the water evaporates, then reduce the heat and continue cooking until they are golden brown.

**Onions brown more quickly** if you add a little sugar to the pan when frying.

**Before adding onions to a stuffing**, always part-cook them as the stuffing will never reach a high enough temperature to cook them thoroughly.

## Oranges and Lemons

**A juicy orange gives** approximately 60 ml (4 tbsp) juice and a juicy lemon gives about 45 ml (3 tbsp) juice.

*'Get more juice out of a lemon ...'*

---

**Get more juice out of a lemon** by warming it slightly before squeezing.

**Always grate the rinds of oranges and lemons** before squeezing. It's easier than trying to grate a flabby shell.

**If you don't own a zester**, use a potato peeler to remove rind from oranges and lemons.

**Oranges peel more easily**, pith and all, if put in a hot oven for a few minutes first.

**To add just a drop of juice to a mixture**, pierce one end of a lemon or orange with a cocktail stick and squeeze out the juice you require. Keep the hole stopped up with the stick until you need a little lemon or orange juice again.

**Store lemons** in a polythene bag. They will keep for one week at room temperature, 6 weeks in the fridge.

83

**Add leftover grated lemon or orange rind** to a jar of caster sugar and use it to add flavour to cakes and puddings.

**Lemon juice prevents discoloration** of some fruit and vegetables. Squeeze over sliced apples and bananas when making fruit salad, and add to the cooking water of apples, cauliflower and Jerusalem artichokes.

**Use lemon to get rid of persistent smells.** Add a slice to the liquid when cooking fish, and rub the cut surface of half a lemon over a wooden chopping board after chopping onions.

**Lemon juice can be used instead of vinegar** in most recipes, but not when pickling.

**Pasta**    **Stop pasta bubbling over when cooking** by putting a knob of butter or a tablespoon of oil in the water. This also helps prevent the pieces sticking to each other.

**Remember that** spaghetti and macaroni double in bulk when cooked, but noodles only swell by about a quarter.

**When cooking fresh pasta**, remember that it takes only about 5 minutes to cook compared with the 10–15 minutes needed for the packeted variety.

**Cook pasta** without a lid on the pan to prevent it going soggy. It should be served *al dente,* i.e. it should still have some bite in it.

**Pastry**    **For extra light pastry**, add a little lemon juice to the water when mixing.

**To make pastry easier to handle** and 'shorter' when cooked, leave it to 'rest' before rolling it out. Cover it and put it in the fridge for about 20 minutes.

**Pastry that's too crumbly to roll out** can be made into a crumble topping. Break it up with a fork and add grated cheese for a savoury dish and sugar and spice for a dessert.

**A batch of dry rubbed-in pastry mixture** will keep for several weeks in an airtight container in the fridge. To use, allow it to come to room temperature and add water as usual.

**Avoid stretching pastry when rolling out** as this will result in shrinkage during baking.

**To get the optimum rise from flaky pastries**, bake on a damp baking sheet.

**Brown glazed pastry** by adding a pinch of salt to the beaten egg.

*'A knob of butter helps prevent pasta pieces sticking to each other.'*

**Prevent the edges of a flan over-browning** by covering them with thin strips of kitchen foil before cooking.

**After lining a flan dish or ring**, don't trim round the edge with a knife. Run a rolling pin across the top and the surplus pastry will fall away neatly.

**Use up leftover pastry trimmings** by making them into biscuits. Knead some desiccated coconut and caster sugar into the pastry scraps. Roll out, cut into fingers or rounds, place on a baking sheet and bake until golden brown and crisp.

**To stop a pastry flan case going soggy**, brush it with egg white before baking 'blind'.

**Flans baked in glass and earthenware dishes** tend to have soggy bases. Improve this by standing them on a pre-heated metal baking sheet when cooking.

**You need 100 g (4 oz) pastry** to line a 15-cm (6-inch) flan tin, 150 g (5 oz) to line an 18-cm (7-inch) flan tin, 200 g (7 oz) to line a 20.5-cm (8-inch) flan tin, 250 g (9 oz) to line a 23-cm (9-inch) flan tin, 300 g (11 oz) to line a 25.5-cm (10-inch) flan tin, and 350 g (12 oz) to line a 28-cm (11-inch) flan tin. Fluted flan *rings* are deeper than fluted flan *tins*, so use a size larger tin for a recipe that specifies a ring.

**If a pastry case for a sweet flan breaks**, put 60 ml (4 tbsp) jam in a small pan, boil and brush well into the broken edges. Press together and brush over the join again with more melted jam. Allow to cool before filling the repaired flan case.

**Refresh savoury pastries, flans or quiches** by heating them in the oven at 160°C (325°F) mark 3 for 5-10 minutes, according to the size and quantity.

**Peaches**  **To skin a peach easily**, pop it into a pan of boiling water and count to 15 before removing and peeling it. Use a potato peeler on really firm ones.

**Peppers**  **To skin peppers**, char them under a hot grill, turning constantly, until the skin blackens and blisters. Plunge them straight into cold water, then rub off the skins.

**Pineapple**  **Core fresh pineapple slices quickly** by pressing firmly over the core of each slice with a small round pastry cutter.

**Pizza**  **Make a quick pizza** using a plain scone mixture as a base. Top the pizza with canned tomatoes, grated cheese, mixed herbs and anchovies, if liked.

**Porridge**  **To make the porridge pan easier to clean**, melt a knob of butter or margarine in it before making the porridge.

**Potatoes**  **New potatoes don't store well.** Never buy more than 3 days' supply at a time.

**To make scraping new potatoes easier**, soak them in warm water for a few minutes beforehand.

**To save scraping new potatoes**, rub the skins off after boiling when they come away easily, or eat them in their skins.

*' Before frying potatoes,
dry them thoroughly...'*

**For really crisp roast potatoes**, rough the
surfaces with a fork after boiling for 7 minutes.

**Speed up the cooking time of baked potatoes**
by pushing a metal skewer through the middle
of each one.

**Before frying potatoes**, dry them thoroughly to
prevent spattering.

**For really creamy mashed potatoes**, use a
hand-held electric mixer to mash the potatoes
in a saucepan on the hob. Watch out for non-
stick coatings though.

**Use instant potato mix** to thicken soups and
stews quickly.

**Prawns**  **There are 20–25 prawns in 600 ml (1 pint).**
They yield about 75 g (3 oz) when peeled.

**Preserves**  *See* **Jams and Preserves**

**Raspberries**   **Avoid washing fruits like raspberries** and strawberries unless absolutely necessary as this can cause loss of flavour. If you must wash it, put the fruit in a colander and run cold water through.

**Recipe quantities**   **When doubling the quantities in a recipe,** remember that you don't necessarily need to double the amount of seasoning needed, or the time the dish takes to cook. Use the given amount of seasoning and check the taste before adjusting it. If the dish is not cooked by the time stated, continue cooking, testing from time to time, until it is cooked.

**Rhubarb**   **Reduce the acidity of rhubarb** by cooking it in cold tea.

**Rice**   **Rice trebles in quantity when cooked.** Allow 50 g (2 oz) per person.

'*Rice trebles in quantity when cooked.*'

**Rice can be cooked up to 3 days in advance** and stored in a covered container in the fridge. To reheat, place in a roasting tin, dot with butter, cover with foil and place in a pre-heated oven at 180°C (350°F) mark 4 for 30–40 minutes. Fork through after 15 minutes.

**Salads**  **Stop salad going soggy** by placing an inverted saucer in the base of the salad bowl. This stops the dressing forming a pool. You should only dress a salad *just* before serving, taking care not to use too much dressing.

**Don't wash a wooden salad bowl** or the wood will become dry and may crack. Wipe it out with kitchen paper after use. Rub a little vegetable oil on the outside and the inside from time to time to maintain its sheen. Store it with a clean piece of kitchen paper inside to prevent dust settling on the slightly oily surface.

**Use up crisp leftover vegetables** to make a salad to serve as a starter or with cold meats. For the best flavour, toss the vegetables in French dressing while they are still warm and chill well.

**Salt**  **To prevent salt going damp**, keep a few grains of rice in the jar.

**Sandwiches**  **When making mounds of sandwiches**, cream the butter in an electric mixer, then combine it with the filling. This cuts the amount of spreading you have to do by half.

**If you have to prepare sandwiches each day**, make up some big batches and freeze them, packed in meal-size quantities. Take one out of the freezer at breakfast and it will be thawed by lunch. Avoid putting salad and egg fillings in the sandwiches, however, as they don't freeze very well.

**If you haven't got a sliced loaf** and you want to make a lot of sandwiches, cut the loaf lengthways. This gives the same number of sandwiches but doesn't involve so much spreading.

**Stop sandwiches going soggy** by putting wet ingredients like mustard, mayonnaise and tomato between slices of meat and cheese so they don't come into contact with the slices of bread.

## Sauces

**Correct a lumpy sauce** by straining, whisking or whizzing in a blender.

**If a Hollandaise sauce curdles** because of over-heating, save it by pouring the sauce into a cold bowl and whisking well. Strain if necessary.

**Stop skin forming on a savoury sauce** by covering it with a circle of dampened grease-proof paper.

**Freeze sauces** in ice-cube trays, then store in bags in the freezer. You can then thaw only as much as you need.

**When making a sauce** to serve with canned vegetables, use the drained-off liquor from the can.

**The quickest way to make a smooth sauce** is to combine the ingredients in a blender, then put in a pan, bring to the boil and simmer, stirring, for 2–3 minutes.

**Make sauces for ice cream** from damaged soft fruits. Cut off the damaged parts of the fruits and purée the remainder.

**Use runny jam as a fruit sauce** for hot puddings or ice cream.

**To give white sauce a glossy finish**, add a tablespoonful or two of cream at the last minute, but be careful not to re-boil the sauce.

**Sausages**  **Turning sausages in a frying pan is easier** if you join them in pairs with a cocktail stick.

**Seasoning**  **Remember that freshly ground pepper** has a better flavour than the ready-ground kind. Whole peppercorns store better and for longer. White peppercorns are hotter, black more aromatic, so mix them in the mill to your own taste.

**Make up a jar of seasoned flour** by adding mustard powder, paprika, dried herbs and salt. Store it in a lidded jar and use it for added flavour when coating liver, sausages, chicken pieces or fish fillets.

**Shortbread**  **Before baking shortbread**, lightly oil a wooden shortbread mould to make the cooked shortbread easy to remove without cracking.

**Snipping**  **When snipping sticky things,** like marshmallows or dates, dip the scissor blades into hot water from time to time to stop them sticking.

**Soup**  **Over-salty soup is improved** by the addition of a little sugar. Alternatively, add more liquid

'Turning sausages in a frying pan
is easier if ...'

and some diced vegetables, such as potato
and carrot, and simmer until cooked.

**Spices**    *See* **Herbs and Spices**

**Steaming**    **When steaming in an aluminium pan**, add a
little acid (vinegar, a slice of lemon or some
apple peel) to the water to prevent the pan
discolouring.

**Make a steamed sweet pudding special** by
shaking a little demerara sugar round the inside
of the bowl after greasing. This will give it a
delicious toffee-like crust.

**Stock**    **If you haven't time to make stock**, store bones
in a polythene bag in the freezer until you
have.

**Freeze stock in ice cube trays** so you don't
have to thaw a large block when you only
want a small quantity.

**To save freezer space**, reduce stock for freezing to a concentrated form by boiling in an uncovered pan to evaporate the surplus liquid.

**Storing**  **Don't add new dry goods** on top of old ones as the old may spoil the new.

**Save space in the fridge or freezer** by using square or rectangular storage containers rather than round ones.

**Straining**  **When straining fruit** it is better to use a nylon mesh sieve than a wire one which might taint or discolour the fruit.

**Sugar**  **Soften hard brown sugar** in a microwave oven in seconds. If you haven't got a microwave oven, cover the sugar with a thick damp cloth and leave it overnight.

**Sweetcorn**  **Cook sweetcorn cobs** lightly in *unsalted* water as salt toughens the kernels.

**Syrup**  **To weigh syrup easily**, first lightly flour or grease the scale pan. This allows the syrup to slide off without sticking.

**Tomatoes**  **Ripen green tomatoes** in a warm, dark place with a ripe tomato in amongst them.

**When flavouring a dish with tomato** paste or purée, compensate for its acidity by adding a pinch of sugar or a teaspoonful of honey or redcurrant jelly.

**Extract the very last bit of tomato paste** from the tube with a rolling pin.

**Weights and Measures**

**One egg white** weighs about 25 g (1 oz). **One egg yolk** weighs about 25 g (1 oz). **One whole egg** weighs about 50 g (2 oz).

**A Size 4 egg** is roughly equivalent to the old standard sized egg.

**To measure small quantities accurately**, use standard measuring spoons rather than tablespoons and teaspoons. Metric and imperial measuring spoons are available.

**15 ml (1 tbsp) syrup** weighs approximately 25 g (1 oz).

**A 15-cm (6-inch) flan** takes half as much filling as a 20.5-cm (8-inch) flan; an **18-cm (7-inch)** flan takes half as much as a 23-cm (9-inch) flan and a **25.5-cm (10-inch)** flan holds twice the amount of filling in a 20.5-cm (8-inch) flan.

'Extract the very last bit of tomato paste from the tube...'

**When using dried yeast**, remember that 15 g ($\frac{1}{2}$ oz) or 15 ml (1 tbsp) is equivalent to 25 g (1 oz) fresh yeast.

**Yogurt**    **Make an instant milk shake** by whisking half a small carton of fruit flavoured yogurt into a glass of cold milk.

**Add natural yogurt to cooked dishes** just before serving. Although the flavour will not change, overheating may spoil the appearance of the finished dish.

**Use natural yogurt instead of single cream** in sauces and dressings. It's cheaper and contains fewer calories.

# Indoor Gardening

**Bottle gardens**

**When filling a carboy** with charcoal and compost, use a chute of rolled stiff paper. Tilt the carboy or the tube of paper to direct the charcoal and compost where you want it.

**To make planting holes in the compost** in the bottom of a carboy, lash a small spoon or lolly stick to a stick. Ram the plants into place with a cotton bobbin wedged on to the other end of the stick.

**Start off a bottle garden** with tiny, slow-growing plants so that the bottle does not become full of foliage too quickly.

**Bulbs**

**Store bulbs** packed into old nylon tights or stockings. Hang them up so that the air can circulate around them.

**After planting a bowl of indoor bulbs**, scatter some grass seeds over the soil to provide an attractive background. for the flowers when they come up. If the grass grows too tall, trim it with scissors.

**Remember to plant bulbs** with no air space underneath them or they may rot.

**Most bulb fibre** must be thoroughly moistened before use. The simplest way to do this is to punch several holes in the plastic bag and immerse it in a bucket of water until the fibre is soaked. Squeeze it almost dry through the fingers before using.

**When bulbs have finished flowering**, allow the leaves to dry off naturally before removing the bulbs for storing. Put the bowl somewhere out of sight until they are ready for storage. Alternatively, plant bulbs such as hyacinths and tulips in a sheltered spot outdoors until foliage dies down and lifting can take place.

**When planting bulbs in pots indoors**, cover small bulbs completely with compost or bulb fibre, but leave the tips of large bulbs exposed. In both cases, allow room for watering.

**Start bulbs off** in a cold dark place, but do not bring them from a cold shed into a warm room—this inhibits their growth. Acclimatise them gradually.

**Cut flowers**   **Help cut flowers to last longer in water** by trying the following tricks. Find one that works for you and stick to it.

Put a few drops of bleach or dissolve a soluble aspirin in the water

Add a pinch of salt to the water

Snip the ends of the flower stems off at a sharp angle

Cut a little more off the stems each day

Crush woody stems before putting them into water

Sear hollow stems with boiling water before arranging them

Change the water in the vase every couple of days

Keep a piece of charcoal in the water

Spray the flower heads with a light mist of water each day

Stand cut flowers overnight in a bucket of cold water up to their necks before arranging.

**Cut flowers for arranging** in the evening. They build up their food supply during the daylight hours and the more food they contain when cut, the longer they will last. Failing this, cut them in the early morning when cool and wet.

**If your children bring you a posy** of very short-stemmed flowers, make an attractive arrangement in a shallow dish by tucking them in between a layer of pebbles placed in water. Seashore pebbles are usually a good shape and size. Wash them first.

**Stop tulips drooping in an arrangement** by piercing the stems through with a pin just behind the flower heads. This releases the air bubble in the stalk which prevents them absorbing water.

**Keep a buttonhole flower fresh all day** by singeing the end of the stem with a match after standing it in water overnight.

'Keep a buttonhole flower
fresh all day...'

**To make cut roses last longer**, steep them in cold water up to their necks for an hour or two and hammer the stems at the base before arranging. Positioning the vase out of direct strong sunlight will also help.

### Cuttings

**Plants make very nice gifts.** Take cuttings from your herbs and other plants, sow seeds and plant bulbs in time for them to grow big enough to make Christmas or birthday presents.

**When taking pot plant cuttings**, use a thick knitting needle or pencil to make holes in the soil for them.

### Everlasting flowers

**Flowers can be dried in a microwave oven.** Colour and appearance remain good and the flowers last just as well as when dried by more conventional methods. Many microwave oven manufacturers supply instructions for this in their manuals.

**When picking flowers for drying**, gather them on a warm dry day when there is the minimum amount of water on them. Flowers picked when wet will not dry satisfactorily.

**For best results when drying**, choose flowers which have not yet come into full bloom.

**It is easier to arrange many dried flowers** if they have a malleable stem. Make a false stem out of florists' wire. Before the flower is dried, cut off the natural stem to within 1 cm ($\frac{1}{2}$ inch) of the flower head. Bend a small hook in one end of a piece of wire and insert the long straight end through the flower centre, pulling it down through the flower neck so that the hook is embedded in the flower centre. As the flower dries, it will shrink and tighten firmly round the wire. Cover the wire with coloured florists' tape.

**Fruit trees**   **You can grow some fruit trees in pots** to stand on your balcony or patio. Choose varieties grown on special dwarf rootstock, where appropriate.

**Hanging**   **Make an unusual hanging basket** from half a
**baskets**   coconut shell. Make three holes at equal distances round the rim and thread string or wires through.

**Water plants in hanging baskets carefully** as the soil tends to dry out quickly.

**To reduce watering**, place moss over the compost between plants. A lining of polythene will help retain moisture and reduce dripping.

' Make an unusual hanging basket...'

**Herb gardens**

**Make an attractive herb garden** for your patio in an old porcelain sink. Water will drain through the plug hole.

**For a winter's supply of mint**, bring a root or two inside. Pot it up in good compost.

**Speed up the germination of parsley** by pouring hot water on the seeds before sowing.

**Patios**

**For a more decorative patio,** fix plant pots or window-boxes securely to the top of a wall and grow trailing plants down it.

**Plant pots and Containers**

**When using baskets to stand plant pots in**, put a foil dish or piece of kitchen foil in the bottom first to prevent the basketwork becoming sodden and deteriorating.

**If you're potting up plants in pretty containers**, don't worry if they have no drainage holes. Cover the base with a good layer of pebbles or crocks and mix a few pieces of charcoal in with the soil. Provided you don't overwater, the plants should drain satisfactorily.

**Look for unusual containers for house plants** in junk shops and at jumble sales.

**Mobilise tubs and large pots** on the patio by putting them on a castor base. This enables the tubs to be wheeled around to catch all available sun.

**Potting**

**Always buy a good potting compost.** It is a false economy to use soil lifted from the garden for potting indoors unless it can be sterilised and then mixed with other ingredients into a proper compost.

*' Look for unusual containers...'*

**All composts should be moistened before use**, but never made sodden. To test, take a handful and squeeze lightly. It should hold together in a loose ball, but fall apart easily when handled.

**To assist drainage from pots**, put pieces of charcoal or broken china in the bottom.

**Don't discard cracked terracotta flower pots.** When smashed into small pieces, they make useful 'clinker' to put in the bottom of whole pots since they absorb moisture and keep the soil damp as they dry out slowly.

**Before refilling old clay pots** with new soil, scrub and soak them thoroughly to get rid of possible soil infection.

**To help retain moisture in flower pots**, mix some used tea leaves with the soil when potting.

**If, when repotting houseplants**, some soil becomes lodged on the leaves, brush it off gently with a clean paint or pastry brush. Do not let the leaves get wet.

**When making holes for plants**, be sure that they are large enough to allow the roots to lie naturally, and that plants are set at the same depth as before.

**Save the flat sticks from ice and other lollies** to use as markers in pots and bowls.

**To avoid pricking your fingers** when potting a cactus, use a sling of folded paper to support the plant and assist in repotting it.

**Pot plants**     **Keep plants away from** oil heaters and gas appliances.

**Plants don't like smoke**, so remove them from the room if you're expecting a group of smoking guests.

**To provide constant humidity for a plant**, stand the pot inside a larger pot. Pack peat

' Plants don't like smoke...'

between the pots, water the peat and keep it moist all the time. Another method is to rest the plant pot on a saucer of small pebbles and water, but make sure the water doesn't touch the pot.

**No plant likes** a big change in temperature from day to night.

**Increase humidity and keep leaves clean** by spraying your plants regularly with a fine mist of water from a plant spray, but don't spray water on to hairy leaves, especially in strong sunlight.

**Don't leave plants** in front of a window on cold winter nights unless there is double glazing or a heavy curtain between the plants and the window, and never leave your plants between a window and the curtain at night or anywhere where they might be in a draught.

**Don't put plants** on top of a radiator—they'll get too hot and dry out.

**Most plants like short periods outdoors** in the summer if the sun isn't too strong, but don't put them out if they're in flower.

**Plants breathe through their leaves** so they need to be clean. Wipe large leaves on both sides with a damp cloth or moistened cotton wool. Clean soft, hairy leaves with a small artist's brush. Plants with this kind of leaf should not get wet.

**Encourage further blooming** of pot plants by removing flowers as soon as they are dead and thus preventing seeds forming.

**To prevent indoor plants leaning** towards the light, turn them round regularly, even every day if possible.

**When buying houseplants**, avoid market stalls and shops which display them outside. The change from outdoor to indoor conditions can cause them to wilt and die. Watch out, too, when buying plants from heated shops as they then have a chilly journey to your home. Wrap them up well in several layers of newspaper.

**To prevent palms growing too large**, keep them in small pots and repot only when the pots are plainly full of roots.

**Don't use detergent or oil** on plant leaves to make them glossy as these will damage the surface. Water does the trick satisfactorily.

**To encourage bushy growth**, pinch out shoots where they grow away from a leaf by breaking the stem between thumb and fingernail.

## Seeds and Seedlings

**Seeds and seedlings can be raised indoors.** Even those needing high temperatures for germination will grow on a sunny window-sill if they are grown inside polythene bags.

**Make small seeds easier to spread** by mixing them with fine sand.

**Seeds germinating in a dark place** should be inspected twice a day. As soon as they have germinated they should be brought out into the light.

**Seedlings must be grown** as near to a window as possible if they are not to become drawn. Turn them daily once they are in the light to promote even growth.

**Use glass jam jars as substitute cloches** when sewing seeds. Sew three seeds under each jar and, after germination, pinch out the two weakest. Remove the jar before the seedling gets too big.

**Plant acorns** close together in trough-shaped containers to grow a miniature oak forest.

**Tools**   **Buy the best tools you can afford**, preferably stainless steel. They last longer as they don't rust and you're more likely to take care if you've spent a lot on them!

**Always clean tools thoroughly after use.** Have a box of sand handy to dry them off after cleaning. Keep a paraffin-soaked cloth sealed in a polythene bag by a rubber band or twist tie round the top to wipe over tools before you put them away.

**Keep small garden tools**, such as scissors, secateurs, etc., in the compartments of a plastic shoe tidy hung in the shed or garage.

**If you have no tools**, improvise with old cutlery, lolly sticks, etc., and wear gardening or rubber gloves so you can use your hands.

**Watering**   **Test to see if a plant's thirsty** by pressing the soil with a piece of newspaper. If the paper becomes damp, the soil is moist enough. As a general rule, it's best to let the soil become almost dry before watering a plant again. Never pour on a little water each day.

**The best way to water very thirsty plants** is to stand the pots in a bucket of water so that the rim of the pot is submerged. If the soil is dry, you will notice bubbles rising to the surface, fast at first, then less and less frequently. When they cease altogether, remove the plant from the water. Allow the pot to drain before replacing in its usual position.

**If you think you've overwatered a plant**, stand the pot on several thicknesses of newspaper so that excess water can be drawn from the pot. Let it become very nearly dry at the roots before watering it again.

**The best thing to use for watering** is a long-spouted can as it allows you to reach under the leaves of plants and avoid wetting them.

**Check if azaleas or ericas need watering** by the colour of the stem. When the plant has sufficient water, the stem shows dark brown. When only 1 cm ($\frac{1}{2}$ inch) of wet stem shows above the soil level, the plant needs watering again.

**If leaves of plants turn yellow or drop off**, this could well be the result of too much watering, or the plant may have been affected by fumes from a gas fire, boiler or cooker.

**When watering plants like cyclamen**, avoid wetting the corms as this could cause rotting. Always water from the bottom.

**Tap water is fine, but rain water is even better.** Put plants outdoors in summer showers.

**When you go away** and there is no one to water your plants, stand them round a bucket of water in a safe place. Tie a small stone to one end of a long wick and drop it into the bucket. Push the wick's other end into the compost in one of the plant pots. Do one wick for each plant and make sure the wick is wet and working properly before leaving.

**Avoid overwatering house plants** by standing them in a saucer of water. They will suck up only as much as they need.

**Avoid watering tender plants** with cold water from a tap by keeping a can of water permanently in a sunny place.

**An empty washing-up liquid bottle** is ideal for watering indoor plants. The nozzle will direct the water where you want it to go. Make sure it is well washed out before use.

**Self-watering pots are not suitable** for plants needing only a little moisture as they keep the compost too moist.

**If houseplant compost has dried out** and shrunk, water it by standing the pot in a bucket of water filled to just below the level of the pot rim. Soak it for 30 minutes, then drain thoroughly.

## Window-boxes

**To keep a window-box moist**, cover the soil with a layer of gravel. This will also help prevent soil being spattered over surrounding woodwork or glass when you water or when it rains heavily.

# Safety First

**Chemicals** | **Never decant chemicals** of any kind into a different container. Even the most firmly fixed labels can come off and you won't remember what the contents are. Decanting into drinks' containers is particularly dangerous.

**For extra safety**, store poisonous garden chemicals, etc., in their containers in a large screw top bottling jar. Fix a clear 'poison' label on the outside.

**Many aerosol and adhesive products** used in the home contain strong solvents which are flammable and can be toxic if inhaled. Always use them in a well ventilated room where there is no naked flame, and do not smoke. Wear protective gloves and goggles.

**Do-it-yourself sense** | **When doing electrical repairs**, always remember to switch off the mains' electricity and remove fuses.

**Always wear goggles to protect your eyes** when drilling or chiselling at brickwork.

**Wear a mask when doing dusty jobs**, especially in confined spaces.

**When working with a hammer and chisel**, wear strong gardening gloves to protect your hands from blows.

**Only use the right tool for the job.** Never try and 'make do' —it will only lead to accidents.

111

*'Always read and follow the directions...'*

**Always read and follow the directions** for the use/operation of DIY equipment and products before using them.

**Keep children away from DIY work areas** and tools and keep chemicals of all kinds out of their reach.

**Emergency first aid**

**If a serious accident has occurred**, send for a doctor or ambulance. Move the patient as little as possible.

**To help relieve pain** from a wasp or bee sting, apply an antihistamine cream, surgical spirit or a solution of bicarbonate of soda. If none of these is available, try the cut surface of an onion. If the sting is left in the wound, remove it carefully with a pair of tweezers.

**When a cut or wound bleeds profusely**, remove any obvious foreign bodies, then apply a sterile dressing and cotton wool or a clean pad, and bandage the wound firmly. **For a nose bleed**, press firmly on the soft part of the nose and breathe through the mouth. **For bleeding from a varicose vein**, raise the leg and apply firm pressure with a dressing.

**Keep a small first aid kit in a kitchen cupboard** as this is where most home accidents are likely to occur.

**If a poisonous cleanser or disinfectant** has burned the mouth, do not make the patient vomit. If conscious, gently give plenty of milk or water to drink and get medical aid urgently.

**If poisonous berries or tablets** have been swallowed, lie the patient down with his head turned to one side. Seek medical aid urgently and save any berries, tablets or vomit to identify poison.

**Burning clothes** should be smothered by covering the flames with cushions, blankets or rugs. Do not remove clothing from burned areas as it is usually sterile. Douse burned or scalded areas with cold water until cool, then cover with a dry sterile dressing. Give sips of water if the victim is conscious.

## Fire precautions

**Keep a fire blanket** hanging near the cooker in the kitchen.

**A small domestic fire extinguisher** on each floor of the house could save lives. Make sure they are checked regularly.

113

'Fit a smoke detector . . .'

**Fit a smoke detector in your home** to give an early warning of fire. Large houses and those on several floors will need more than one detector Check them weekly to ensure they are functioning correctly.

**Hygiene** **Always store dry foods** sealed in containers (airtight if necessary) to prevent possible contamination by insects or vermin.

**Cutting raw meat or poultry on a board** can leave traces of bacteria. After washing thoroughly, rub the board over with a household bleach solution and rinse well before draining or drying. Never buy cooked meat from the same counter from which the butcher is serving raw meat. Be careful never to put unwrapped cooked and raw meat together in the fridge or anywhere else, as this can lead to cross-infection by bacteria.

**Always wash salad ingredients** and peel or wash fresh fruit.

**Wash your hands before touching food**. Change the kitchen hand towel regularly or use paper towels.

**Before handling food**, cover a cut or sore on your hand with sticking plaster or spray-on plastic dressing (available from chemists).

**Ensure that cooked foods are cooled quickly** before refrigerating or freezing to prevent bacteria breeding.

**Pay attention to 'sell by'** and 'best eaten before' dates on food. They are there for your protection.

**Food that is left out most of the time**, like a sugar bowl, should be covered to keep off flies and dust.

**Never eat food which** appears or smells off in any way.

**Cans of food with dents or bulges** should be thrown out.

**Avoid putting dirty clothes** (If you do laundry in the kitchen) or cleaning cloths on work surfaces or the draining board.

**Soak kitchen cloths**, scouring pads, washing-up brushes and mop heads in a bleach solution regularly.

*'Ensure that family pets remain in good health and that strict hygiene is observed...'*

**Ensure that family pets remain in good health** and that strict hygiene is observed in regard to them.

**Insist on the family washing their hands** before meals and after going to the lavatory.

**Keep the lavatory hygienic** by washing the flush handle and seat of the lavatory once a week with a bleach solution. Don't forget to do any taps and the door knob as well. Rinse thoroughly and dry.

**If rubbish collection is infrequent**, burn what you can and bury the rest.

**Use bin liners in your kitchen bin** and seal them with a twist tie when full.

**Avoid keeping a dustbin near** the kitchen door, if possible.

**To help young children to remember** to use the same towels and toothbrushes, give them each a complete set of everything in the same colour.

**If you run out of toothpaste, use salt** to clean your teeth.

## Medicines

**Store medicines and pills in a locked cabinet.**

**When taking antibiotics or other medicines** that need to be taken regularly, set an alarm clock to ring when the next dose is due.

**Don't keep medicants** after the patient has recovered, but take all surplus tablets and medicines to your nearest chemist for disposal.

## Safety

**When cooking,** keep long handles on pots and pans turned inwards rather than protruding into the room.

**Don't polish floors too highly** or have slippery rugs on them. Loose rugs can be attached to a special backing which stops them sliding around (or see page 36).

**Use a non-slip mat in the bath,** especially if you have elderly people in the household.

**Teach children never to eat anything growing** and keep houseplants out of their reach.

**Use mats, not tablecloths, for children's meals.** They're much easier to wipe clean and can't be pulled off so easily.

**To stop children poking things into** electric wall sockets, fit them all with covers, or keep dummy plugs in them.

**A child can drown in even very shallow water,** so fix netting securely over a garden pond or ornamental pool.

**Fit safety catches on all windows** out of which a child could fall.

**Block off stairs with a safety gate** until a small child is able to cope with them safely.

**Always lock a garden gate** so that children cannot stray on to a road.

**When a child has outgrown a large playpen**, use it yourself to do the ironing in as this decreases the risk of the child pulling the iron off the board and burning himself.

**Never leave containers of hot liquid**, such as saucepans and coffee pots, where children could reach them, and store matches, scissors, knives and other sharp objects in drawers or cupboards that they cannot open.

**To prevent a baby slipping around in the bath**, put a flannel or small hand towel in the bottom.

**Do not keep cleaning products** under the sink or anywhere that a child could reach them.

**Always lock the garden shed**, especially if there are small children in the family. Apart from the hazards of chemicals, there is the risk of them cutting themselves on sharp tools.

**Double electric wall sockets** avoid the temptation to use adapter plugs which can be dangerous, so if you are having a new socket fitted, or when re-wiring, have double sockets fitted.

# Metric Measurements for Cooks

## CONVERSION TO METRIC MEASUREMENTS

The metric measures in this book are based on a 25-g unit instead of the ounce (28.35 g). Slight adjustments to this basic conversion standard may be necessary when making some recipes to achieve satisfactory cooking results.

If you want to convert your own recipes from imperial to metric, we suggest you use the same 25-g unit, and use 600 ml in place of 1 pint, with the British Standard 5-ml and 15-ml spoons replacing the old variable teaspoons and tablespoons. These adaptations will sometimes give a slightly smaller recipe quantity and may require a shorter cooking time.

Note   Sets of British Standard metric measuring spoons are available in the following sizes — 2.5 ml, 5 ml, 10 ml and 15 ml.

When measuring milk it is more convenient to use the exact conversion of 568 ml (1 pint).

For more general reference, the following tables will be helpful.

METRIC CONVERSION SCALE

| | LIQUID | | | SOLID | |
|---|---|---|---|---|---|
| Imperial | Exact conversion | Recommended ml | Imperial | Exact conversion | Recommended g |
| ¼ pint | 142 ml | 150 ml | 1 oz | 28.35 g | 25 g |
| ½ pint | 284 ml | 300 ml | 2 oz | 56.7 g | 50 g |
| 1 pint | 568 ml | 600 ml | 4 oz | 113.4 g | 100 g |
| 1½ pints | 851 ml | 900 ml | 8 oz | 226.8 g | 225 g |
| 1¾ pints | 992 ml | 1 litre | 12 oz | 340.2 g | 350 g |
| | | | 14 oz | 397.0 g | 400 g |
| For quantities of 1¾ pints and over, litres and fractions of a litre are used. | | | 16 oz (1 lb)   453.6 g 1 kilogram (kg) equals 2.2 lb. | | 450 g |

Note Follow either the metric or imperial measures for all ingredients in recipes as they are not interchangeable.

## OVEN TEMPERATURE CHART

| °C | °F | Gas mark | °C | °F | Gas mark |
|---|---|---|---|---|---|
| 110 | 225 | ¼ | 190 | 375 | 5 |
| 130 | 250 | ½ | 200 | 400 | 6 |
| 140 | 275 | 1 | 220 | 425 | 7 |
| 150 | 300 | 2 | 230 | 450 | 8 |
| 170 | 325 | 3 | 240 | 475 | 9 |
| 180 | 350 | 4 | | | |

# Roasting Tips and Times

**Beef** Allow 20 minutes per 450 g (1 lb) plus 20 minutes if the meat is on the bone; 25 minutes per 450 g (1 lb) plus 25 minutes if the meat is boned and rolled. Put the meat in a roasting tin with the thickest layer of fat uppermost and the cut sides exposed to the heat. Cook at 220°C (425°F) mark 7 uncovered, basting from time to time with the juices from the tin. For a more moist joint, cook more slowly at 190°C (375°F) mark 5, allowing 27 minutes per 450 g (1 lb) plus 27 minutes for joints on the bone; 33 minutes per 450 g (1 lb) plus 33 minutes for boned and rolled joints.

**Chicken/Capon** Brush the chicken with melted butter or oil and sprinkle with salt and pepper. A few strips of fat bacon may be laid over the breast to prevent it from becoming too dry. Put in a shallow roasting tin and bake in the oven at 200°C (400°F) mark 6, basting from time to time and allowing 20 minutes per 450 g (1 lb) plus 20 minutes. Put a piece of greaseproof paper over the breast if the flesh shows signs of becoming too brown. Alternatively, wrap the chicken in foil before roasting; allow the same cooking time, but open the foil for the final 15–20 minutes to allow the bird to brown.

**Duck** Sprinkle the breast with salt and pepper. Cook in the oven at 190°C (375°F) mark 5, allowing 30 minutes per 450 g (1 lb).

**Lamb** Put the meat in a roasting tin with the thickest layer of fat on top and add dripping if the joint is very lean. Cook at 220°C (425°F) mark 7, allowing 20 minutes per 450 g (1 lb) plus 20 minutes. If the joint is boned and rolled, allow 25 minutes per 450 g (1 lb) plus 25 minutes. Baste the joint from time to time with the juices from the tin.

**Pheasant** Cover the breast of the bird with strips of fat bacon. Roast in the oven at 230°C (450°F) mark 8 for 10 minutes, then reduce the temperature to 200°C (400°F) mark 6 and continue cooking for 30–40 minutes, according to the size of the bird, basting frequently with butter. About 15 minutes before the cooking time is completed, remove the bacon, dredge the breast of the bird with flour, baste well and finish cooking.

**Pork** Score the rind and rub with oil and salt to give crisp crackling. Cook at 220°C (425°F) mark 7, allowing 25 minutes per 450 g (1 lb) plus 25 minutes if the meat is on the bone; if the meat is rolled it is better cooked at 190°C (375°F) mark 5 for 30–35 minutes per 450 g (1 lb) plus 35 minutes. Pork should never look pink when cooked.

**Turkey** For the quick oven method, cook at 230°C (450°F) mark 8 covered with foil; for the slow method, cook at 170°C (325°F) mark 3 without foil. Before cooking, spread the bird with softened dripping or butter or cover the breast with strips of fat bacon.

| *Weight* | *Slow* | *Quick* |
|---|---|---|
| 2.7–3.6 kg (6–8 lb) | 3–3½ hours | 2¼–2½ hours |
| 3.6–4.5 kg (8–10 lb) | 3½–3¾ hours | 2½–2¾ hours |
| 4.5–5.4 kg (10–12 lb) | 3¾–4 hours | 2¾ hours |
| 5.4–6.3 kg (12–14 lb) | 4–4¼ hours | 3 hours |
| 6.3–7.3 kg (14–16 lb) | 4¼–4½ hours | 3–3¼ hours |
| 7.3–8.2 kg (16–18 lb) | 4½–4¾ hours | 3¼–3½ hours |
| 9–10 kg (20–22 lb) | 4¾–5 hours | 3½–3¾ hours |

With the slow method, if the bird almost fills the oven, it may be wise to protect legs and breast with a piece of foil. Unless the bird is cooked in foil, baste it regularly, turning it round once to ensure even browning. Foil, if used, should be unwrapped for the last 30 minutes, so that the bird may be well basted and then left to become crisp and golden.

**Veal** Cook at 220°C (425°F) mark 7 for 25 minutes per 450 g (1 lb), plus 25 minutes if the meat is on the bone. If the joint is boned and rolled, allow 30 minutes per 450 g (1 lb) plus 30 minutes. Baste or cover with bacon rashers.

# How Many Rolls of Wallpaper are Needed?

Standard wallpapers come in rolls *approximately* 10.05 m (11 yards) long and 530 mm (21″) wide. The following chart will help you estimate the number of rolls you need.

Figures show you number of rolls required

| WALLS Height from skirting | Distance around the room (doors and windows included) | | | | | | | | | | | | | | | | | |
|---|---|---|---|---|---|---|---|---|---|---|---|---|---|---|---|---|---|---|
| | 30′ 9 m | 34′ 10 m | 38′ 12 m | 42′ 13 m | 46′ 14 m | 50′ 15 m | 54′ 16 m | 58′ 17 m | 62′ 18 m | 66′ 19 m | 70′ 21 m | 74′ 22 m | 78′ 23 m | 82′ 24 m | 86′ 26 m | 90′ 27 m | 94′ 28 m | 98′ 30 m |
| 7′–7′ 6″ 2.15–2.30 m | 4 | 5 | 5 | 6 | 6 | 7 | 7 | 8 | 8 | 9 | 9 | 10 | 10 | 11 | 12 | 12 | 13 | 13 |
| 7′ 6″–8′ 2.30–2.45 m | 5 | 5 | 6 | 6 | 7 | 7 | 8 | 8 | 9 | 9 | 10 | 10 | 11 | 11 | 12 | 13 | 13 | 14 |
| 8′–8′ 6″ 2.45–2.60 m | 5 | 5 | 6 | 7 | 7 | 8 | 9 | 9 | 10 | 10 | 11 | 12 | 12 | 13 | 14 | 14 | 15 | 15 |
| 8′ 6″–9′ 2.60–2.75 m | 5 | 5 | 6 | 7 | 7 | 8 | 9 | 9 | 10 | 10 | 11 | 12 | 12 | 13 | 14 | 14 | 15 | 15 |
| 9′–9′ 6″ 2.75–2.90 m | 6 | 6 | 7 | 7 | 8 | 9 | 9 | 10 | 10 | 11 | 12 | 12 | 13 | 14 | 14 | 15 | 15 | 16 |
| 9′ 6″–10′ 2.90–3.05 m | 6 | 6 | 7 | 8 | 8 | 9 | 10 | 10 | 11 | 12 | 12 | 13 | 14 | 14 | 15 | 16 | 16 | 17 |
| 10′–10′ 6″ 3.05–3.20 m | 6 | 7 | 8 | 8 | 9 | 10 | 10 | 11 | 12 | 13 | 13 | 14 | 15 | 16 | 16 | 17 | 18 | 19 |

CEILINGS     To calculate the number of rolls required, work out the square area in metres and divide by five

N.B. The larger the pattern, the more material you need to allow for matching. Ask the retailer's advice.

## SYMBOLS

The Wallpaper Marketing Board has now recommended the progressive introduction of these international performance symbols. They are now beginning to appear in wallpaper pattern books and on product labels.

| | | | | | |
|---|---|---|---|---|---|
| 〜 | spongeable | ⌐ | strippable | ⌐ | offset match |
| ≈ | washable | ⌐ | peelable | $\frac{50_{cm}}{25}$ | design repeat distance offset |
| ≋ | super-washable | ⌐ | ready pasted | ⏐) | duplex |
| ▬ | scrubbable | ⌐ | paste-the-wall | ≋ | co-ordinated fabric available |
| ☼ | sufficient light fastness | →‖° | free match | ↑ | direction of hanging |
| ☼ | good light fastness | →‖← | straight match | ↑↓ | reverse alternate lengths |

Information supplied by the Wallpaper Marketing Board

# A Guide to Washing and Cleaning Care

## INTERNATIONAL TEXTILE CARE LABELLING CODE

| Symbol | Washing temperature | | Agitation | Rinse | Spinning Wringing |
|---|---|---|---|---|---|
| | Machine | Hand | | | |
| **1** 95 | very hot (95°C) to boil | hand hot 50°C or boil | maximum | normal | normal |
| **2** 60 | hot 60°C | hand hot 50°C | maximum | normal | normal |
| **3** 60 | hot 60°C | hand hot 50°C | medium | cold to minimize creasing | short spi or drip d |
| **4** 50 | hand hot 50°C | hand hot 50°C | medium | cold to minimize creasing | short spi or drip d |
| **5** 40 | warm 40°C | warm 40°C | maximum | normal | normal |
| **6** 40 | warm 40°C | warm 40°C | minimum | cold to minimize creasing | short sp do not ha wring |
| **7** 40 | warm 40°C | warm 40°C | minimum do not rub | normal | normal sp do not hand wri |
| **8** 30 | cool 30°C | cool 30°C | minimum | cold to minimize creasing | short sp do not hand wri |
| **9** 95 | very hot (95°C) to boil | hand hot 50°C or boil | minimum | cold to minimize creasing | drip dr |
| | **Do not machine wash** (the appropriate hand washing instructions are usually given alongside this symbol) | | | | |
| | **Do not wash** at all | | | | |

*Fabric*

for white cotton and linen articles without special finishes, this process provides the vigorous washing conditions. Wash temperature can be up to boiling (100°C) and tion and spinning times are maximum. Ensures good whiteness and stain removal.

cotton, linen or viscose (rayon) articles without special finishes where colours are fast 0°C. Provides vigorous wash conditions but at a temperature which maintains fast urs.

white nylon or white polyester/cotton mixtures; less vigorous than either 1 or 2. The temperature (60°C) is high enough to prolong whiteness, and cold rinsing followed ort spinning minimizes creases.

coloured nylon; polyester; cotton and viscose (rayon) articles with special finishes; lic/cotton mixtures; coloured polyester/cotton mixtures. Except for washing temperature ical to process 3. The lower, hand hot temperature (50°C) safeguards the colour and finish.

cotton, linen or viscose (rayon) articles where colours are fast at 40°C, but not at 60°C, process has warm wash (40°C), maximum agitation, normal spinning or wringing. The wash temperature is essential to safeguard colour fastness.

those articles which require low temperature washing, (40°C) minimum agitation, a rinse and a short spin eg acrylics; acetate and triacetate, including mixtures with wool; ester, wool blends. These conditions preserve colour and shape and minimize creasing.

wool, including blankets, and wool mixtures with cotton or viscose (rayon); silk, which s low temperature washing (40°C) and minimum agitation but requires normal spinning. hing in this way preserves colour, size and handle. Do not hand wring or rub.

ilk and printed acetate fabrics, with colours which are not fast at 40°C, requiring to be ed at a very low temperature (30°C), with minimum agitation and spinning. Unlikely pear on UK produced goods.

cotton articles with special finishes which benefit from a high temperature (95°C) wash equire drip drying. Again rarely to be found on UK produced goods.

### WASHING TEMPERATURES

| | | | | |
|---|---|---|---|---|
| Boil | Self-explanatory | 50°C | Hand-hot | As hot as the hands can bear. |
| Very hot | Water heated to near boiling temperature. | 40°C | Warm | Pleasantly warm to the hand. |
| Hot | Hotter than the hand can bear. The temperature of water coming from many domestic hot taps. | 30°C | Cool | Feels cool to the touch. |

## BLEACHING

 This symbol indicates that household (chlorine) bleach could be used. Care must be taken to follow the manufacturer's instructions.

 When this symbol appears on a label household bleach must *not* be used.

## IRONING

The number of dots in the ironing symbol indicates the correct temperature setting—the fewer the dots the cooler the iron setting.

cool                 warm                  hot                   do not iron

## DRY-CLEANING

The letter in the circle refers to the solvent which may be used in the dry-cleaning process, and those using 'coin op' dry-cleaning should check that the cleaning symbol shown on the label is the same as that in the instructions given on the front of the machine.

 Goods normal for dry-cleaning in all solvents.

 Goods normal for dry-cleaning in perchloroethylene, white spirit, Solvent 113 and Solvent 11.

 May be dry-cleaned professionally. Do not 'coin op' clean.

 Goods normal for dry-cleaning in white spirit or Solvent 113.

 Do not dry-clean.

## DRYING

Care labels may also include one or other of the following symbols recommending a particular drying method.

 Tumble drying beneficial but not essential.

 Do not tumble dry.

124

# Index